WE ARE NOT INVISIBLE

Twenty-six women veterans from varied branches of the service share the enlightening stories of their lives before, during, and after their military service

D1081878

S. FABIAN BUTALLA

HELLGATE PRESS   ASHLAND, OREGON

WE ARE NOT INVISIBLE
©2019 S. FABIAN BUTALLA

Published by Hellgate Press
(An imprint of L&R Publishing, LLC)

Hellgate Press
PO Box 3531
Ashland, OR 97520
email: sales@hellgatepress.com

Cover & Interior Design: L. Redding
Cover Photo: Dallas Smith

Library of Congress Cataloging-in-Publication Data available from the publisher on request

ISBN: 978-1-55571-953-1 (paperback)

ISBN: 978-1-55571-954-8 (ebook)

Printed and bound in the United States of America
First edition 10 9 8 7 6 5 4 3 2 1

This book is dedicated with gratitude to the twenty-six women veterans who were willing to share their life stories before, during, and after their military experiences...

and to the women who have served and are now serving in all branches of our country's Armed Forces.

In Memoriam

Bridget Mary Cronin
September 12,1968 - March 17, 2019

Those who knew and loved Bridget Cronin will forever hold her in
our memories with great respect. It is with deepest gratitude to this
amazing, talented woman, without whose creative genius and selfless
service which she devoted to assisting, promoting, and honoring
women veterans, this book would not exist.

Contents

Acknowledgments

S EVERAL DEDICATED WOMEN have been instrumental in the creation of this book, beginning with Bridget Cronin, Founder and Executive Director of the Ars Bellum (Arts of War) Foundation in St. Paul, MN.

Ars Bellum provides evidence-based art therapy for veterans dealing with PTSD, and has developed a specific women-only program for veterans who have experienced military sexual trauma (MST).

Ars Bellum joined forces with the Women Veterans Initiative, the 23rd Veteran, and the Minnesota Department of Veterans of Foreign Wars Charitable Association, which provided funding for this project.

In June 2017, Bridget attended the National Association of Women Veterans Coordinators held in Minneapolis, where she learned of a public awareness campaign being held in the state of Oregon, called "I Am Not Invisible" (IANI). The campaign involved a traveling display of professional, poster-sized photographs of several women veterans from various branches of the service, who have joined the group called IANI ("I am Not Invisible") because they feel or have felt that feeling of "invisibility" regarding their military service. The photographs are presented on large easels and they can fill a conference hall.

Bridget enthusiastically enlisted the aid of other women veterans organizations, and she was assisted from the start by Army veteran Angie Batica, who became the spokeswoman for the Women Veterans Initiative.

Professional photographs of the individual women veterans who were involved, as well as group photos, were fully the work of Twin Cities photographer Dallas Smith. The display traveled throughout the state of Minnesota in 2018.

The goal of the campaign is to shine a spotlight on women veterans whose contributions, experiences, and needs are too often ignored, or overlooked socially, politically, and legally. Many face significant barriers and challenges in accessing health care and other services while also experiencing a lack of recognition unlike their male counterparts.

"We want to increase awareness and conversation about the broad spectrum of experiences women veterans have had—both good and bad—and we want women veterans to know they are recognized, they are honored, they are supported." One of the key goals of the project and statewide tour was to connect women veterans to the local community-based resources (and groups who do support them and can provide practical help for women veterans if they know who they are).

First contact with the author of this book came in May, 2018, when Sandra Fabian Butalla visited the display in Chisholm, MN, and was immediately struck with a feeling of respect and honor toward the women depicted in the photographs.

Much credit must be given to former Marine Sergeant Chris Magnusson. She was monitoring the exhibit the day author Sandra Butalla first viewed the display. Chris, who is currently the Regional Librarian for the Arrowhead Library System, based in Mt. Iron, MN, a board member for the Women Veterans Initiative and several community and veterans' organizations, contacted others in the IANI group, and Sandra became involved.

A great deal of assistance was provided by Col. Laura Ludwig, who served as the liaison between Sandra and the IANI women veterans. Her rapid response to questions and tasks was invaluable in the production of the manuscript for this book. She is very dedicated and involved in numerous women veterans organizations. Her enthusiasm and contributions to this book are inestimable and greatly appreciated.

Photographer Dallas Smith has donated the copyright privileges and permission to print her wonderful photographs and front cover photography for use in this book, and for that we are most grateful.

Poet/musician Sarge Lintecum has also donated copyright privileges and permission to print his poignant and stirring poem titled "Invisible

Soldier" for use in this book, and it is a perfect addition for which we are honored.

I am greatly indebted to the women veterans who have agreed to share their stories in this book.

The twenty-six women veterans whose stories comprise this book, and I will be forever grateful to the late Bridget Cronin for her inspiration, creativity, and devotion to helping women veterans.

Technology assistance by Dustin Miller of Tech Bytes in Eveleth, MN was greatly appreciated during the preparation of the manuscript for this book.

My deep gratitude goes to Hellgate Press for their acceptance of this manuscript for publication. Their guidance was invaluable and their patience was limitless.

WE ARE NOT INVISIBLE

Introduction

*T*HAT WOMAN WHO just passed you on the street. The lady who lives down the block. The girl sitting next to you on the bus. The mother of those two children at the park. Your grandmother. Your own mother...any or all of them may very well be or have been veterans. Most of them have rarely, if ever, talked about their service to our country. Many families have been totally surprised to learn that a female family member has served in the US military.

There are more than 29,000 women veterans in the state of Minnesota alone, and no doubt, similar numbers in many other states around the country. They are everywhere, and like their male counterparts, they too have served in America's military. Most of them left their homes and families around eighteen years of age and were sent for training all over the U.S. before being transported to faraway places with sometimes dreadful conditions or the horrors of war. But they were part of something much bigger than themselves, and they were well-trained for the jobs they performed. Regardless of their assignment, it was crucial to the U.S. military machine, and they were needed. Yet, many rarely, if ever, talk about it.

When they returned to civilian life, having left their friends from the service, the job they specialized in, and the structure of military life after several or many years, they they could no longer wear their uniform,, which was for each of them, their identity. Try to imagine the reality of what it is like to try to fit back into their former life or to try to create a new path. For many, re-integration as a civilian was and still is one of the primary causes of Post-Traumatic Stress Disorder (PTSD), which plagues so many veterans.

Twenty-six American women were eager to share their true-life stories.

Each of their stories comprises a unique chapter, as her life unfolds. Their first-hand portrayals of the negative struggles and positive rewards of their service to our country has been a pleasant journey down "Memory Lane" for many of these women. For some others, it forced them to dredge up their long-held traumatic memories that in a way proved cathartic as it was no longer lodged deep inside, and at last prompted a few to seek professional help, which has turned into something very positive for them.

These noble women have served in several branches of the military throughout the United States and in countries around the world. They have joined together in a group called "I Am Not Invisible" because they all share the common hope that their stories may inspire others who, like themselves, have experienced a feeling of "invisibility" regarding their military service, and to enlighten the general public who remain, on the whole, unaware of the service rendered by our American women veterans.

Preface

*T*WENTY-SIX WOMEN, each with a different story, yet with some similarities. Their backgrounds vary, as do their life experiences, but they all have one thing in common—they all left their homes and families at an early age and willingly entered into the military service of their country.

Browsing through the daily newspaper one northern Minnesota spring day in 2018, I noticed a picture of a woman as part of an article. Looking closely, I saw that it was actually a photo of a "poster-sized picture" of a woman, and it appeared to be on an easel for display. The article provided details of a traveling display titled "I Am Not Invisible," which was touring the state of Minnesota. Its purpose was to promote awareness of the contributions that women veterans have, and still are, making to the United States military.

As the author of two published books (*The Man Who Fell to Earth*, and *Warbirds in the Cloak of Darkness*), both of which are true life stories of Minnesota Airmen who had amazing and highly dangerous experiences during World War II, naturally I was interested in how and why the women veterans in the display came together. The article mentioned there were more than thirty, and it provided dates and locations where it could be viewed. My curiosity was aroused and a few days later, I went to the Minnesota Discovery Center located in Chisholm, MN.

I was directed to the large second-story hall. Circling the perimeter of that room were tall easels, each of which supported a 2'X3' professional photo of a different woman. They were alike in that each woman was wearing black. There was a sentence or two below every photo, identifying the woman, and briefly describing her military service.

I walked slowly around the room, stopping in front of each picture. They all looked happy. It appeared that the group had served in most all branches of the military. Some were young, others were still actively serving, and there were those who had completed their service some time ago. I was so focused that it wasn't until I reached the last easel when I realized how quiet it was in the room. I was lost in my thoughts of each of these women and the sacrifices they have made for our country. Then I was immediately struck by the sobering recognition that I was alone in the large hall. No one else was there to view that powerful display.

At that point I was greeted by Chris Magnusson, the woman in charge of monitoring the event. She had sat without a whisper behind a table in the far corner of the room, allowing me to view the entire display uninterrupted. We introduced ourselves. Chris explained the purpose of the "I Am Not Invisible" initiative, and I was both impressed and saddened to think that any woman who has served our country should ever feel that her service was overlooked or dismissed. Case in point—I was the only visitor in the room at that time.

I told Chris about my two published books and I said that someone should write a book about these women. She was instantly excited about that suggestion, and even more so when I added, "Each woman's story could be a chapter in the book."

Needless to say that one thing led to another, and the wheels began to turn. Then others involved in the initiative contacted me and offered to assist in any way. I simply could not turn my back on them, and I threw my hat in the ring, knowing that I may be able to help them in promoting awareness of the service of all women veterans.

Thus began my journey into the lives of twenty-six of the women pictured in the traveling display.

It has been my honor to interview, collect, and organize the stories of each of the wonderful women who were willing and able to share their experiences. Any departure from the truth or actual facts by any of them or myself is purely unintentional.

All of the stories which are told by the women in this book are as they recall them. Some may make you smile.

Some may make you sad.

Some may shock you.

Together, their stories may enlighten and inspire those who endeavor to read them.

WE ARE NOT INVISIBLE

ONE

Corinne Anderson

SSgt Corinne Anderson
US Air Force, 1997-2002

I WAS BORN on August 3, 1977, and grew up in a very small South Dakota town named Carthage.

My parents divorced when I was around five years old. My mother dealt with domestic violence in her first marriage, which affected my view of the world at a young age. My mother remarried and worked three jobs. Alcoholism, workaholism, and violence definitely influenced my desire to strive to be healthy, educated, and prosperous.

My upbringing helped me to become very independent and resourceful. I went to the University of South Dakota for a year after high school, but I was not satisfied with student loans and a lack of direction. I dropped out of college and went to Colorado Springs to move in with my cousin.

As time passed, we had shared ideas about what our next steps would be. I was reminded of my own declaration, made out loud during my senior year that "I was going to join the Air Force and move to Hawaii." My cousin Dawn and I had both thought previously on our own about joining the military. We both wanted higher education, but we did not want to go into a lot of debt. We were adventurous and loved to travel, and we felt that we had the support to follow through with our decisions at that time.

I had another female cousin who had joined the Army, and a few uncles who had served in Viet Nam. After exploring other branches of the military, I still was leaning towards the Air Force. I heard that the Air Force was the hardest to get into, and it had the best sleeping quarters and food. I felt that it was the right fit for me, and my cousin agreed.

My family was pretty shocked when they heard the news of our decisions, and my mother was nervous, but Dawn and I were accepted by the USAF and off we went to Basic Training in Texas.

We arrived at the base in San Antonio on December 3, 1997, and we were pleased that it was clean (as some were reported to be not so.)

Training was a blur! I remember waking up five minutes prior to revelry almost every day, then scrambling to get going! There was lots of running, an abundance of yelling, and no sugar for the first five weeks. After the five weeks were up, I retaliated by drinking two Cokes and a few candy bars in a short time. I soon paid the price by suffering the unpleasant effects of sugar overload, and had no one but myself to blame.

Our ASVAB (Armed Services Vocational Aptitude Battery) test score determined what we would be qualified for in our military duty. Dawn and I joined "open general," meaning we didn't know what training we would be going to prior to joining. I heard that the California reservists had a year-long waitlist in the area of Video Production, which I was very interested in. Needless to say, I was extremely happy when I learned that it was my assignment. Dawn was sent to Texas, then to Japan.

I was sent to technical school at Ft. Meade, MD., where it was five months of pushing to the limits. We ran at 3:30 a.m. three times a week, and had cleaning requirements plus eight hours of class a day. It was extremely exhausting and expansive at the same time. I have never been pushed so hard in my life!

We learned lighting, audio, video recording and editing. Back in the day, they didn't expect us to be a journalist as well. We were fortunate to have some fun with our creativity during that period of physical, emotional, and mental challenges.

My senior high school declaration that I would join the Air Force and move to Hawaii manifested itself four years after I had graduated. A guy I knew told me that there was a position open in Hawaii and I must apply for it. I somehow just knew that I was going. I was at my mother's house when the letter arrived, informing me that I did, in fact get the assignment. My mom was nervous about my going, but I was screaming with joy! The Air Force was sending me for a three-year special duty assignment there from 1999 to 2002.

When my plane landed in Hawaii and I walked outside, I was greeted with the smell of flowers. I didn't know there was a place that looked or smelled like Hawaii. I loved it!

Unfortunately, my video training wasn't utilized much there. The war in Iraq had started and I dealt more with secure briefings for staff and executive level officers.

During my free time, I was able to go sailing, snorkeling, hiking, deep-sea fishing, and I tried surfing. Although I was afraid of heights, it was on my Bucket List to try sky-diving. One day I did it! Then I didn't sleep for a week.

I was never deployed outside of the United States.

I wasn't sure if I was going to stay in the military after my first tour of duty. I was on the fence. As it turned out, a coworker of mine was in the Pentagon on September 11, 2001 when it was hit by a plane. Afterward, I had a lot of anxiety about reenlisting. The fear of the unknown and terrorism so close to home had really worn on me during my last year in the service. I thought about cross-training into another field, but I ultimately decided to give civilian life a go with the college money I had earned from the military.

I feel that I gained a lot of personal growth during my military service from Boot Camp to Advanced Training, then my time served in Hawaii. Having been raised in a small town, I was exposed to different cultures while in the service. I learned discipline and a work ethic. While in Hawaii, I was doing my best to be my best. I knew I would have to strive to be on my own if I left the military, and I could not fail. I needed money for school, and at the time, I had no back-up plan. I did leave the service and spent eight months soul-searching at my mom's house in South Dakota.

I did not want to work in video production, as I had done in the service, because commercial software was different from that of the military, and I felt that I no longer possessed the skill set necessary.

I went to school at Aveda Institute, then worked as a makeup artist for Estee Lauder for a year. After that, I got a job working in the travel industry for two years and worked technical support for nine years with the help desk and online technical support.

I eventually went to Metropolitan State University in St. Paul, MN, where I completed my Communication degree. I am currently working as a contractor in tech support for HVAC.

I am proud to have served my country. I realize that everyone joins the military for different reasons, but in the end, every one is serving their country. I made a decision to join the military for multiple reasons: education, travel, and patriotism. Women make up a small percentage of the military, so it does make some sense why we are not as noticed. Males have been dominant throughout human existence. We really need to have a voice for women. Empowerment and awareness are only going to strengthen society's perception toward the treatment and equality of women.

My message to other women veterans who have felt or who are feeling a veil of "invisibility" regarding their military service is this: We live in a time where women have the most opportunity ever! It's only going to get better from here on.

Eleanor Roosevelt had some of the most inspirational quotes that resonate with me (and hopefully with you too.) Here are a few of them:

"No one can make you feel inferior without your consent."

"You must do the things you think you cannot do."

"You gain strength, courage and confidence by every experience in which you really stop and look fear in the face. Then you are able to say to yourself, 'I lived through this horror. I can take the next thing that comes along!'"

TWO

Susanne Aspley

Sergeant First Class Susanne Aspley
US Army Reserve, 1983-2005

I HAD A WONDERFUL childhood, growing up in Scottsbluff, Nebraska. I spent a lot of time outside. My dad would pile my brother and me, along with our two bulldogs, Spike and Fritz, in the car, and he would take us to Roubideox Pass, where he taught us how to shoot a bow and arrow and a shotgun. I drove minibikes up and down the roads between ditches with my brother. We climbed Chimney Rock, hiked the Wildcat Hills, and ran up and down Scottsbluff National Monument.

In the late '70s my dad worked as a country doctor at the county hospital, and my mom was an RN. My dad worked days, 7:00-3:00 a.m., and my mom worked 3:00-11:00 p.m. So, it was always my dad, my brother, and I when we got home from school. One stormy night when we should

5

have been safely in the basement, we begged my dad until he gave in and pushed us up on the garage roof to watch a tornado with binoculars, and it was spectacular! By the time my mom got home from work, the tornado had passed, and we were all safely asleep.

The fall of 1979 was difficult for me as my dad got a better job offer and our family moved to Minnesota. I started ninth grade at Minnetonka, and I hated it. It was horrible being a farm kid moving to a different community, especially at that age. I couldn't wait to graduate from high school and leave.

Four years later, I did just that. I chose to join the Army Reserve because they offered the job I wanted—photojournalist—and they had a great college benefit: the GI Bill.

I was inspired to join the military by several relatives who themselves had served over the years. I am a descendant of a Revolutionary War vet, and the tradition continued as my grandfather was in WWI and my uncle in WWII. My father served during the Korean War and my brother joined the Marines. I wanted to be part of something bigger than myself, and the military provided that. My family and friends were very supportive of my decision.

Two weeks after high school graduation, I left for Basic Training at Fort Jackson, South Carolina, which lasted from June-August of 1983. My drill sergeant told us, "You join the military for one of two reasons. You are either running from something, or you are looking for something." I guess I was doing both.

One time during Basic, I was assigned KP duty for the day. At the end of the evening, I went into the freezer and took a delicious frozen cheese-cake that unfortunately turned out to be for the general's retirement party the next day! I sneaked back to the barracks and ate the entire cheesecake in the latrine stall.

At 5:00 a.m. the following morning during PT (exercises), as I was doing sit ups, I rolled over and puked out the entire cheesecake! My staff sergeant asked what was wrong. I told him what I had done. He made me do more sit ups.

Another time I was supposed to climb up a rope, run across the rafters, and jump into a sand pit. I was trying to climb the rope and my drill sergeant was encouraging me until I told him, "I can't!" He got so mad at me, and screamed, "Never say the word 'CAN'T!' Get up that God damn rope now!" I was up that rope, across the rafters, and down in the sandpit before I realized I could do it!

After my Basic Training, I was sent to Fort Ben Harrison, outside Indianapolis, for Advanced Training. I attended PSYOPS school (Psychological Operations) at Fort Bragg, North Carolina, and NBC school (Nuclear, Biological, Chemical Warfare) at Fort Carson, Colorado. My first six years in the Reserve I was with the 13th PSYOPS as a journalist. But I never worked in NBC, which is probably a good thing because I am terrible with math! (Blast-radius-wind direction-wind speed—argh!)

I also trained at numerous places throughout my career—all over the U.S., as well as in Panama and Honduras.

When my contract was up with the Army, I got my Bachelor's degree from the University of Minnesota in 1988, and was accepted into the Peace Corps for two years in Thailand. I served in a small fishing village from 1989-1991. I was assigned to community development, and I taught English to school children. I worked on small projects like a duck farm and well digging.

In 1997, I rejoined the Army Reserve and served as a photojournalist again. I deployed to Bosnia (1997), twice to Kuwait (1998 and 1999), and to Guantanamo Naval Base (Gitmo) Cuba (2002).

While deployed, I handled media interest in the Islamic detainees arriving at Gitmo and helped manage the media in Kuwait during the "No Fly Zone" years of 1998 and 1999, as well as public affairs in Bosnia.

At the end of my service in the 88th Army Reserve Command, the last few years were absolutely horrible because of the MST (Military Sexual Trauma) which I was subjected to and reported, but no one believed me. The man eventually went to prison on a different charge of child rape/trafficking charge, but it was pure hell because everyone refused to believe me.

I retired in 2005 after serving twenty non-consecutive years. I am now a writer, and my website is *aspleywrites.com*.

***

In spite of the tribulations I faced in my final years while in the military,

I am proud of my service and would do it all over again in a heartbeat. I feel "invisible" as a veteran, but I didn't serve for the public accolades. I served because I loved the people I was with, and I love my country.

My message to other women veterans who have felt or who are feeling a veil of "invisibility" regarding their military service is this: It happens all the time, but don't take it personally. Most people don't overlook us because they think we are less than men, only because they are not used to women in the military. They simply need a reminder that women do indeed serve.

I also want all veterans to know that there is help if you are struggling. You are not alone.

Keep that hope—and yourself—alive.

THREE

Patricia G. Baker

LTC Patricia G. Baker (Ed.D.)
US Army National Guard, 1992-2019

I WAS RAISED as a farm kid. My parents were living near the southwest Minnesota town of Garfield when I was born on January 4, 1975 in the nearby town of Glenwood. I was the first of three daughters born to Norm and Ann Baker. We lived on multiple farmsteads due to my dad's work as a farmhand when I was growing up.

Although we lived in a tiny house surrounded by an almond grove in California when I was four years old, it was the only time we did not live in Minnesota during my childhood. When I was school age, we moved from farmstead to farmstead due to the depressed farming economy of the 1980s. When the farmers could not afford to pay my dad, he would have to move us to another town to find work.

From Head Start as a four-year-old in California to sixth grade at Walnut Grove, we moved five times to five different farms and five different school districts. By then my sister Amy had been born almost three years after me in late 1977. She was four months premature and had growth and health issues during her entire childhood. In 1981 my sister Jessica was born, and she was a carbon copy of me. At that time, we were living on a farm outside of Jeffers, MN.

We received every kind of government assistance for our family of five, including free school lunches, heating assistance, food assistance, free athletic fees, hand-me-down clothes from other farmers' wives, as well as assistance from local churches and civic groups.

Across the quarter lived the Schoppers who had milk cows and three boys the same ages as me and my sisters. My parents would go to their house to play cards, or sometimes go over to the Pankonin's and bring us with for cards night.

I loved being a farm kid. It appealed to my sense of adventure and my independent streak. What was really great about being in the Storden-Jeffers school district was the year I turned eight I could join 4-H. At eight I was not only a farm kid who went to school with other farm kids and rode the bus with other farm kids, but I got to join a 4-H club with other farm kids (called the "Amboy Sunrisers"). That first summer of 4-H was instrumental for me as it was the doorway into civic duty, countywide competitions, and submitting projects at the county fair.

The first year I participated in the Cottonwood County Fair was farm kid nirvana in 1983. My lambs won ribbons for showmanship, my sewing project won ribbons, and even my photography project did well. Some things stick with you for a lifetime, including my first chance to publicly compete in the county 4-H speech competition, where I shared top honors in the speaking contest. Across the years of moving from farm to farm, the consistent threads were 4-H and school. Although we moved often, our family would join the 4-H club in the new township and become members in each county. From Cottonwood, to Laq Qui Parle, to Redwood, the Bakers were in 4-H clubs across southwest Minnesota.

As for school, I learned to love it thanks to my second grade teacher, who showed me the art of writing in cursive, phonics, and three-digit addition and subtraction, and I reveled in it! Then in the fourth grade at Sanborn, my teacher saw academic potential and had me enrolled in the Omnibus Program for academically advanced students. It was my first chance to do self-paced study on a Commodore computer and my first exposure to a book that intrigued me—*The Narnia Chronicles: The Lion, the Witch, and the Wardrobe.*

From the Omnibus Program, there was no looking back academically for me. I spent the rest of my formative years on the farm focused on academics and 4-H. Then, in 1987 we moved to the tiny town of Revere—located on Highway 14 with a population of just 117. There I finished my days in secondary school and the years leading up to my enlistment in the Minnesota National Guard as a soldier.

My decision to join the military was mostly influenced by my dad in very subtle ways from the periphery. He rejoined the military in the mid-1980s after a significant break in service post-draft for Viet Nam. I would see him return from drill weekends in battle dress uniform and it sparked my interest in military service. He never tried to convince me or "twist my arm," figuratively speaking. He just modelled the behaviors of what it meant to be a soldier and an NCO. I envied his adventures to Honduras and going across the country for military schools and training.

By the age of fifteen, I was perusing the academy brochures in the high school guidance counselor's office. Both the Marines and the Army appealed to me. By sixteen, I had decided that waiting to vie for the academies took too long. I wanted to join the military right away and not wait until after college. I opted for the Army due to the most open military occupational specialties for women.

That cemented my decision to join the Minnesota Army National Guard at seventeen with a signed age waiver from my parents. My high school friends were a little surprised, considering my rather rebellious outward appearance that included piercings and somewhat alternative attire, but my parents and teachers were not surprised at all. I enlisted as a 31L Wire Systems Installer in the Army National Guard.

I knew I was bound for the University of North Dakota, Fighting Sioux

ROTC BN. I departed for my undergraduate studies at the university to pursue an aeronautical degree and FAA pilot's licensure as an aviation major after high school and intended to parlay that into my military career. I did both. After college, I intended to commission as an officer and branch into Army Aviation.

The summer of 1992 found me headed for Basic Combat Training at Fort Leonardwood, Missouri. This training was segregated, hence my entire platoon of C/5-10 was all women. My contract with the Minnesota National Guard was for split training over two summers in order to accomplish Basic in the summer of 1992 and Advanced Individual Training at Fort Gordon, Georgia in the summer of 1993.

From 1992-1995 I served as an enlisted soldier 31L Wire Systems Installer in the Guard. Then at college I took an active duty scholarship with UND ROTC Battalion. I went on active duty with the Army from 1997-2006 as an Army aviator and commissioned officer.

Once commissioned, I was chosen for the Aviation Branch and sent to flight school at Fort Rucker, Alabama, to learn helicopter systems, obtain helicopter flight instruction, and obtain my commercial rotary wing instrument pilot license from the FAA.

As the years passed, I was sent to numerous locations in the U.S. for additional areas of training:

June 1992 – Basic Combat Training (Fort Leonardwood, MO)

June 1993 – Advanced Individual Training -31L (Fort Gordon, GA)

May 1997 – Initial Entry Rotary Wing Course (Fort Rucker, AL)

May 1997 – Aviation Officer Basic Course ((Fort Rucker, AL)

June 1998 – UH-60 Aircraft Qualification Course (Fort Rucker, AL)

April 2000 – Air Assault Course (Fort Campbell, KY)

April 2001 – Aviation Captains Career Course (Fort Rucker, AL)

October 2001 – Command and Staff Services School (Fort Leavenworth, KS)

October 2004 – Cadet Command Recruitment Operations Course (Fort Belvoir, VA)

September 2007 – Public Affairs Officer Qualification Course (Fort Meade, MD)

August 2009 – Phase I Resident ILE (Fort Dix, NJ)

March 2012 – Special Emphasis Manager Course (Patrick Air Force Base, FL)

June 2012 – Equal Opportunity Qualification Course (Patrick Air Force Base, FL)

Aug 2012 – Phase II and III LE (Ft. Dix, NJ) Distance Learning (for promotion to Lt. Colonel)

September 2012 – Equal Employment Officer Course (Patrick Air Force Base, FL)

July 2016 – Aviation Pre-Command Course (Fort Rucker, AL)

January 2017 – Army Small Group Instructor Course (Fort Benning, GA)

January 2017 – Army Basic Instructor Course (Fort Benning, GA)

2019 – War College Fellowship, Tufts, University

My first deployment to Iraq was in March of 2003 at the onset of the war. I was sent to OIFI as a company commander, serving and flying my first combat tour with BRAVO Company, 2-4th Aviation Regiment, 4th Combat Aviation Brigade, 4th Infantry Division (Mechanized.)

I served that first tour in Tikrit, Iraq, at the airfield 8.8 nautical miles from Tikrit palace until March, 2004.

I was the company commander for a fifty-person aviation unit that was charged with flying Command & Control and VIP for the 41D Commanding General. With ten UH-60 Blackhawk helicopters and fifty aviators, crew chiefs and C2 operators in my command, the unit flew combat missions under day, night, and NVGs for one year from Tikrit Airfield. During this tour, I logged 504 hours of combat flight time during thirty-eight named battles and campaigns while assigned to the 4th Inf. Div. (Mechanical).

In May 2008, on my second combat tour to Iraq, I deployed as S4/S8– Senior Logistics Officer, Headquarters and Headquarters Company, 34th Combat Aviation Brigade, Joint Base, Iraq. During that tour, my position on the brigade staff was the oversight of all facilities, equipment, contracts, and the west side of Balad Airfield. As the senior logistician in the brigade, I was charged with the asset management of $1.1 billion in government equipment, funds, and facilities for the 34th Cbt Avn Bde. The 34th CAB was the aviation brigade assigned to Multi-National Force Iraq that was headquartered by the 18th Airborne Corps in Baghdad during OIF Rotation 08-10.

My staff of seventeen subordinates oversaw an aviation brigade that included over 100 airframes, both rotary wing and fixed wing, and over 2,500 soldiers spread out across Iraq on bases from Tallil to Balad.

As a young soldier and officer, I was focused on doing all things that were "hooah." Flying helicopters, going to Air Assault school, and deploying on my first combat tour were all about proving what I was capable of at the 101st Air Assault Division, at the 4th Infantry Division, at Army schools, in Iraq, and in garrison (any assignment as a soldier in the U.S.) As I matured, but especially after my first combat tour, my perspective changed, and it changed markedly. After combat, I stopped and thought about what I wanted to become now that I had lived through war.

Instead of merely what I could do, I thought about what I could become. It had hit me in Iraq that I wanted an advanced degree, so I asked my crew chiefs to help me study (while on breaks between flights) for the GRE (Graduate Record Exam.) I applied to Marquette University from an MWR (Morale, Welfare, and Recreation) tent in Iraq with a computer center and I was accepted as a probationary graduate school student pending acceptable test scores on the GRE upon return to the U.S. I passed.

Once back in the U.S., I started on the path to becoming an academic and role model. I realized there were people that I encountered every day who had never met a woman in uniform and certainly never met a female aviator.

I started to accept speaking engagements for military-themed events and holidays. That snowballed into outreach events that grew into associations and affiliations with groups over the years, such as Global Girls in Aviation, Experimental Aircraft Association, and today as a national board director in the Combat Helicopter Pilots Association.

***

Now as a senior officer (lieutenant colonel), I am focused on my legacy in uniform and how to sway others to become officers and aviators.

Sometimes the slights and stereotypes of others remind me of the work yet to be done to make women in uniform truly visible. I have been stopped at the Minneapolis VA and had others ask if I was lost or remind me that "caretakers are to stay with their veterans while at the VA," or remark that "I did not know that they let women fly in the military."

My response has become much less about being irked, and much more about educating others that women have been able to fly combat aircraft in the military since it officially became policy in 1993. To avoid invisibility, I am now keen to go to events and appointments in uniform, to increase the visibility of all women in the military who currently serve or those who are fellow veterans. I was quick to join the "I Am Not Invisible Initiative!"

> *My message to other women who have or who are now feeling a veil of "invisibility" regarding their military service is this: Don't be blindly sold on the version of the American woman you see on a magazine cover, social media, or an ad on TV. Pretty is fleeting. Celebrity is superficial. No amount of Photoshopping can render the pride that one feels in uniform or the accomplishments that you will obtain as a member of the most elite military that has walked the earth in human history.*

WE ARE NOT INVISIBLE

FOUR

Barbara Barrett

LTJG Barbara Barrett
US Navy Corps, 1967-1969

*M*Y DAD WAS a ship's cook in the U.S. Navy when I was born at
the San Diego Naval Hospital on October 12, 1945. After Dad,
Alvin Beaudin, was discharged in late 1945, we moved with my mother
Wanda to Gilbertville, Massachusetts. There I was raised, along with my
younger sister Marsha and my two younger brothers, Don and Ken.

It was always my plan to become a nurse, work for a year, then join
the Navy. In 1967, I enlisted at the age of twenty-one. My family, especially my parents, were so proud. We were a very patriotic family and
my parents were members of "The Greatest Generation."

In August of 1967 I reported to Newport, RI, where I had already been
commissioned as an ensign when recruited. Navy nurses were spared the

hard Boot Camp, and our training was called "Officer's Indoctrination." During this period, we learned about hospital ships, we were taught Navy terms, and more specifically, how to run a hospital ward full of wounded Marines. We also learned ranks and enlisted ratings.

In September of that year, I reported to the Pensacola Naval Hospital in Florida. I was soon working with wounded Marines, treating their orthopedic and surgical wounds. I did a short time in labor and delivery but soon was back with my Marines. I loved every minute of it!

After the TET OFFENSIVE of 1968, we were extremely busy. There was a Marine that I was taking care of in ICU who had sustained shrapnel injuries from his feet to his hips. He was very ill with an infection and was in an isolation room. We all wore scrubs or isolation gowns in ICU, and when I went in to take care of him, we had many conversations, mainly about how his family and friends would treat him once he was back home in Louisiana. Worried about his disability, he opened up to me about his concerns of finding a job when he got discharged from the Marines. I was his nurse for a few weeks. He said that when he could start eating "real food," he wanted a cheeseburger, fries, and a milkshake.

He gradually advanced to a regular diet. I gave him about a week to make sure he could handle a burger. One day, I went to McDonald's and got him what he wanted. I brought it to the ICU. Before I changed into the scrubs, I knocked on his door. Then I opened it, yelling, "Catch!" as I threw him the bag. I put the milkshake on the table and told him I would be back after I changed into the scrubs. The look on his face was priceless, not only because of the McDonald's meal, but it was the first time he saw me in uniform. He was so surprised because he thought I was a civilian nurse. He said, "Thank you, and I didn't know you were a Ma'am! I hope I didn't say anything that was out of line!" I assured him that he didn't. He never forgot that meal, and I will never forget him.

I eventually ended up being the head nurse in ICU. It was all very fulfilling. However, nothing compared to doing triage with new wounded patients sent to us directly from Viet Nam by the Air Force, and we would say to them, "Welcome home. You are safe."

We had a young Marine who had sustained shrapnel injuries to his neck and esophagus, and now had a permanent tracheostomy. The surgeon who had performed his surgery had such a hard time getting the Naso Gastric tube into his stomach, that he taped a sign on the tube which read: WHOEVER TAKES THIS TUBE OUT DIES! One night, the tube somehow worked its way up and was now in his trachea. He was in severe respiratory distress. The Corpsman on duty called me to come from another ward, and when I got there, I yanked out the NG tube with the note on it. He started breathing and kept mouthing, "Thank you!" And I didn't die!

He had surgery again the next day. That Marine was one of five who had been rescued by Major Stephan Pless, who was awarded the Medal of Honor by President Johnson, and the major would often come to visit my patient, always on the night shift, around 2:00 a.m., so he wouldn't cause a commotion. I would also visit that young Marine after I got transferred to ICU. He was concerned that his girlfriend may not accept him with a permanent trach.

About six months later, he returned to the ICU—to introduce me to his wife, and to say good-bye. He said, "This is the nurse who saved my life." I loved my Marines!

***

I married Roger Barrett, a Hospital Corpsman, in 1968. The following year, my husband received orders to Vietnam. I could not go because they would not allow married couples to be in the same war zone. I had hoped to go on the hospital ship the USS *Repose*, but could not. I was discharged in September, 1969.

After I was discharged, I moved to my home in Massachusetts and lived with my parents for the year that Roger was in Vietnam. I worked in a CCU in a small hospital.

When Roger came home, he mustered out in Boston, and we moved to Minneapolis, where he was from. I worked in ICU at the VA Hospital there for seven years. Then I worked at Abbott Northwestern for twenty-two years in high risk obstetrics. I retired early due to health issues at that time. When I got the OK from my doctors, I returned to work oncall at Fairview Southdale Hospital for about three more years.

During my career as a civilian nurse, I had my share of emergencies, and I loved helping people. But nothing compared to taking care of those wounded Marines who answered our nation's call and paid dearly for it!

Roger and I celebrated our 50th wedding Anniversary in April, 2018. We have two sons and two grandchildren: Gene, his wife, Amy and our grandson, Michael; Jim and his wife, Alison, and our grandson, Ian.

***

I was very proud that I served. I learned to function as part of a team and under stress. It definitely prepared me for a career in high-risk nursing, which I continued to do in the private sector for another thirty-eight years. I believe that those two years in the Navy were my finest hours.

Because of all the war protesting and the rise of the anti-war mentality, I felt "invisible" for many years. Co-workers and friends knew that I had served, but never asked me about it.

The Women Veterans Organizations certainly are working hard to promote our recognition.

My message to young women is this: Consider joining the military. The rewards are endless. Camaraderie is outstanding. You will learn discipline and organization skills while serving and working together.

FIVE

Angie Batica

Specialist Angie Batica
US Army Reserve and US Army, 1992-2000

*I*N THE BEGINNING, I had a normal childhood. However, my parents separated when I was four and divorced when I was six. My mom got custody and we lived with many people and moved every year—sometimes three times a year. We lived with pedophiles, drug dealers, prostitutes, etc.

My mom had a horrible temper. She ended up with a childhood girlfriend and they beat each other up all the time. There was broken glass on the floor, blood on the walls, yelling and screaming, cops at the door.

Her friend had a daughter whom I'd hold to protect. My mom would come home from the bar and start beating me up in the middle of the night (one time when I had a full body cast on due to a broken femur.) It was a nightmare. But it got worse. I was sexually molested by family members and family friends from age four through twelve. Then my mother abandoned me.

Her friend-turned-lover called my dad and I moved in with him. I didn't know him except for occasional visits during holidays. He was very strict and had a bad temper. If I didn't ride my bike or clean perfectly, he'd snap on me. If I said anything, he'd hit me hard. He was angry and depressed all the time. He was a biker on the weekends and a business man during the week. I lived in constant fear. My only escape was drawing. I drew all the time—what I felt, what I saw.

My dad remarried when I was sixteen. My stepmom had three younger kids. I felt like I was being kicked out of the nest. Most of the positive attention and funds went to her and her family. My dad was happier, but I wasn't. I had no contact with my estranged mom during this time. I craved that unconditional love from a mother—and never got it.

My best friend joined the Army Reserves after 11th grade and went to Basic Training during the summer. She was a medic and I was interested in the same field. I couldn't qualify for grants because my parents made too much money and they wouldn't give me a dime. The college offers from the military were hard to pass up. I wanted to leave my life in Minnesota and travel, explore, serve my country with pride, and meet new people. I was naïve, had no direction, and was unsure about my future. I met with the recruiters to see my options, and I decided to join the Army Reserves because of the college funding and because my best friend did.

At seventeen I was in the 11th grade when I waited with a recruiter for my dad to come home from work and forced him to sign the papers. Then I entered the delayed entry program during high school. My family was shocked that a quiet, artistic, feminine, introvert like myself would do such a thing.

I joined active duty because I despised living in Minnesota, trying to make ends meet. I reported to Fort Jackson, South Carolina, in June of 1993 for Basic Training. The following year I was at Fort Eustis, Virginia, which we used to call "Even Uncle Sam Thinks It Sucks." Both locations were hot, full of bugs, and much different from home, although I enjoyed the heat.

When I took the ASVAB (Armed Services Vocational Aptitude Battery), I didn't score well for the medic position, which I had desired. Surprisingly, I qualified high in mechanics. Out of the positions offered, I asked the recruiter which one was most challenging. He said the Aircraft Armament Missile Defense System Repairer, 68J, position would challenge me, so I took it.

Basic Training was fairly easy. After a while, we had West Point cadets take the place of drill sergeants. I got in really good shape and scored high in everything I did. Then there was AIT (Advanced IndividualTraining).

It was six months of hell. The drill sergeants were meaner than any from Basic Training. We were punished every day while going to classes by mean drill sergeants who would make us do fifty push-ups for stepping on a yellow line or they would take away our off-duty privileges for a bad grade, etc.

However, I was learning about mechanical and electrical systems on helicopters, so I was cool with it.

I worked on helicopter armament systems at Ft. Bragg, NC, and at Holman Field in St. Paul, MN.

In 1997-98 I was shipped to Camp Stanton, South Korea, five miles from the DMZ. Again I worked on Cobra helicopter armament systems in the Army Reserves and on Kiowa Warriors. We were always on lockdown and training for war. It was like a prison because we couldn't walk off base. The nearest place we could visit was Camp Casey, an hour away. I received the Army Commendation Medal and Good Conduct Medal.

To tell the truth, my military experience wasn't desirable. It was naturally rough and tough. It challenged me physically and mentally all the time. Above all, I was violently raped, threatened, harassed, and treated as less than dirt by male comrades. I was told multiple times I would be shot if we went to war. Military Sexual Trauma (MST) was "sort of handled" by moving me around, but the violent rape was swept under the rug.

I felt like everything and everyone I believed in let me down. I no longer respected the military and couldn't wait to get out. After being honorably discharged, I returned to my home in Minnesota. I left the service after the six-year requirement in 1998.

It took a real long time for me to come to terms with being a veteran. The transition from military to civilian life was hard. Instead of following dreams to be an actress, I went to a community college and tech school, worked at a liquor store, and lived with my cousin. At first it was great. I was back with old friends, meeting new friends, and partied all the time.

However, I was confused about who I wanted to become and I was lost. People close to me told me I was too old to succeed in acting and I believed them. My stepdad said he'd pay for the last two years of college if I went to business school or something similar. I took some acting classes anyway and he never paid for any college. After ten years, I managed to get a business degree anyway.

Over time, I told my family and friends about the horrible time I had in the Army. None of them understood. They didn't want to hear it. So the painful memories were stuffed inside and buried into my subconscious. I made it a point to demilitarize myself by staying really busy and drinking all of the time.

I remember showing homemade Army videos and the audience couldn't finish watching them. It was too foreign and horrifying to them. Hence began a mission of self-destruction. I was spiraling downward to some very dark places with deviant sexuality, and the urge to hurt men as much as possible, both emotionally and physically.

A few years after leaving the Army, I turned to meth in an attempt to self-medicate. I tried to commit suicide the night before my stepsister's wedding. I started and stopped school and jobs. Every time I pushed my feelings away, they came through the other side. I ended up depressed, jobless, and broke.

Then I started the moving. I relocated all over the country, trying to escape my life. I thought I'd get better but every time I turned around, there I was. My horrible past and behavior followed me. Every time it didn't work out, I'd return back to Minnesota. My family was there. But all of my friends left me. They couldn't handle me anymore. I was truly alone.

In time I got a good job in a food delivery business and worked there for five years. I got new cars and my own house. But the drinking was out of control. Then the trouble with the law happened. It continued happening.

The DWIs, the assaults, and other things piled up. I moved all over the country again. I got arrested again and again. It was a never-ending story.

By 2009 I had a rap sheet longer than anyone I knew. I was a daily drunk and on crack. I had nothing again. I couldn't hold down a job and had no place to live.

After a vicious night with a drug dealer, a booming voice yelled at me, "You better get sober or you are going to die or go to prison!"

At one point, a leader in the VFW told me I might qualify for a VA claim based on what I told him had happened to me in the military. That was in 2005. By 2007 I was 30% disabled, and by 2009 I was 100%.

On July 25, 2009, I put myself into in-patient treatment at the St. Cloud, Minnesota VA—and I have been sober ever since.

I continued to seek all kinds of treatments for my MST, PTSD, depression, addictions, anger, anxiety, and other issues at the VA Medical Center. The VA and Alcoholics Anonymous were my saviors as I worked through all of my issues.

***

I have reconnected with myself and figured out who I am. I have mentored women about their military experiences and/or sobriety. I performed in play called: "Telling: Minnesota and the Moth Storytelling Project," both of which involved several veterans telling their stories of life before, during, and after their military service. It was the first time I publicly discussed my military experience and it was very therapeutic.

Volunteering is now my passion. I hope to inspire other women with it. I was involved with the "I Am Not Invisible Campaign" from day one. I stepped up to help Bridget Cronin, founder of the ARS Bellum Foundation, by recruiting most of the women veterans for this initiative. I was the primary contact with them, including arrangements for the photo shoot, and thousands of emails and texts. I had a part in 80% of the process. It was the biggest project I had ever worked on.

I recently was the Lean In Women Veterans Regional Leader/Chair and Circle Development and Moderator. Twice I served on the board of the Women Veterans Initiative as a Public Media Relations officer and designed their "Women Veteran" license plate.

Other volunteer efforts include Women Veteran National Cohort, Minnesota Special Olympics, Animal Humane Society, Veterans in the Arts, Habitat for Humanity, Goodwill, Feed My Starving Children, ERA Minnesota, The Salvation Army, The Minnesota Humanity Center's Veterans Voices Award Committee, Veteran Resilience Project, DAV, ARS Bellum Foundation Liaison and founder of Veterans of Minnesota community Facebook page. I received the 2013 Veteran Voices Award via the Minnesota Humanities Center.

Currently, I have a position as Administrator for a non-profit called "Service Women Who Serve." It falls under the main non-profit of Women Veteran Social Justice.

I spoke about the "Grassroots Movement as an Individual" at the first Military Women's Coalition Inaugural Meeting in Atlanta on September 11, 2018.

I am a published writer and artist, and instructor. The best part about my life is that in 2013, I got married to my best friend. We have two wonderful children. I love having fun with my family and providing the best opportunities for them. We own and manage a Taekwondo school.

***

When I was discharged from the service, there were no military or veteran posters with women on them. Everything was directed toward men—clothing, VAs, veteran organizations, etc. The general public didn't believe me when I said I was in the Army. Most men didn't like that women served next to them. They treated us with blatant disdain and said we were not real veterans. Society generally seemed to agree.

Many women were sexually assaulted in the service and were not protected. Instead, they were scrutinized, ostracized, and sometimes kicked out. So when we got out, many of us hid. We wrapped ourselves in the "veil of invisibility" because we believed that no one cared about us.

My message for other American women is this: I am sharing this story so others don't go down the same path that I did, even if their "herstory" is awful. I want to share my experience, strength, and hope with others. I want to make a difference in this world and leave it a better place. Women go through the same life events that men do and we are veterans too.

We deserve respect, recognition, and equality. Don't be afraid to speak up!

WE ARE NOT INVISIBLE

SIX

Catherine (Kay) Bauer

CAPT Catherine (Kay) Bauer (O-G)
US Navy (Ret.), 1958-1993

*M*Y PARENTS LIVED in St. Paul, Minnesota, and they wanted a farm and a large family. I was born in October of 1936, the second eldest of their fourteen children. I had seven brothers (one older than me) and six sisters.

As soon as WWII ended in 1945, we moved to a farm near North St. Paul, MN. We had chickens and produce and six newspaper routes. At that time, as soon as we were old enough, we delivered newspapers each morning and evening. We were busy from 3:30 a.m. to 10:00 p.m. every day. Rising before 3:30 a.m., we delivered the newspapers, returned home to feed and water the chickens, helped our mom make breakfast and lunches to take along, went to church, then to school, Monday through Friday during the school year. We ate our breakfast during our first class at school.

Arriving home after school, we changed clothes, delivered newspapers, took care of the chickens again, worked in the produce section of our farm, cleaned up, helped our mom with dinner, ate dinner while discussing the day's events and issues, had thirty minutes of family prayer, helped clear the table and wash dishes, then went out to collect dues (from those on our paper routes and make notes of those who wished to purchase produce, chickens, and eggs.) At that time, the newspapers required those who delivered the papers to pay for them, then attempt to collect from those to whom the papers were delivered. Returning home, we did our homework before going to bed. As the only girl old enough, I also helped Mom darning socks and doing some sewing and ironing.

During the summer we delivered papers, collected for them, worked in the gardens, helped with the multitude of tasks with the chickens and selling them, their eggs, and produce door-to-door.

Each winter our wells froze. We had to collect water every day from a farm several blocks away, using ten-gallon milk containers that a nearby dairy farmer loaned to us. Washing clothes using huge water containers, scrub boards, and hand-turned wringers was a chore! This was even more onerous during the winter when we hung some of the clothes to dry on outside clothes lines. Doing this in the summer was not fun, but easier!

On Sundays we delivered papers only in the mornings, then went to church. After breakfast, we played indoor or outdoor family games, depending upon the weather. We sometimes took short trips in the afternoons after our necessary chores were completed.

I attended a Catholic grade school and a two-year Catholic high school. When I attempted to attend a four-year Catholic school to complete high school, they were not accepting students in their third year at that time. Thus, I attended a public high school for my last two years. I now had to wear regular clothing instead of uniforms. That posed a financial problem for me. I enrolled in a VICA program, which allowed me to get school credit for work. I unsuccessfully attempted to work in a department store where I was required to wear high heels and dressy dresses. I then went to a hospital where they said they would train me to be a nursing assistant. I worked there for two years until they moved the unit in which I worked to a newly-built nursing home. I worked there for another two years before transferring to a hospital.

I had been selected for a four-year scholarship to St. Benedict College. At that time, it was a difficult trip from St. Paul to St. Joseph, MN. The scholarship did not include room and board. I checked out the University of MN but felt I would prefer a smaller college. I met one of the women on my paper route who was graduating from St. Catherine University in St. Paul. After chatting with her, I enrolled at "St. Kate's." My goal since third grade had been to work in the mission field; education seemed to be my way to accomplish that. However, after three years at St. Kate's with a Speech and English major, and primary, then secondary education as a minor, I was not enthralled with this career.

An LPN with whom I had worked at the hospital, convinced me to change my major to nursing. She said I was a very good nursing assistant and would be a great nurse. My fourth year at St. Kate's was spent taking those arduous science and math classes I had thus far avoided. That meant a required 5th year for nursing courses. I then discovered that there were no scholarships or loans for a 5th year!

Since I was financing my education with work, scholarships, and a state loan, this meant leaving St. Kate's without a degree! At that time, I was doing a residency in Contagious Nursing, an area no longer in existence. We cared for polio patients in iron lungs and many wards of patients with tuberculosis, which required us to wear gowns, gloves, and masks.

I was very dejected. A friend, who was a student at the University of MN, stopped by to inquire as to my distress. She said I should accompany her and some other nursing students to the military recruiter's office the following morning, as they had scholarships. The next day found us in a long line in front of the Army recruiter's door. Two of us decided to check out the Air Force. They did not offer scholarships. Then we went to the Navy where the line was much shorter. They offered to pay my tuition, room and board at St. Kate's, plus a monthly salary, which allowed me to pay off my one loan! I was twenty-two years of age. We both joined the Navy in September 1958.

My dad was just as unhappy about my joining the Navy as he was about my choice of nursing. My mom just always asked me if that was what I wanted, and when I replied that it was, she just hugged me and said to do whatever I thought was best for me. Dad always came around to my mom's way of thinking! My friends could not believe that I would go off and into the Navy—by myself!

My first duty station was six weeks of Officer Orientation in Newport, RI. Prior to 1959, the Navy sent medical personnel to their first duty station in their civilian attire and expected that station to orient their new nurses and doctors. These new personnel had unknowingly preferred to purchase uniforms designed for admirals and other senior officers. And, they had no idea about Navy traditions and protocols or when, where, and how to salute.

Therefore, we were the first group of nurses to be assigned to Officer Orientation. We learned about the Uniform Code of Military Justice (UCMJ); ships, aircraft, and weapons; how and what uniforms to wear; marching and saluting; and Navy traditions and protocols. I had a great time and was only on report once—my very first day! I enjoyed having nothing to do except be there. I had been studying for years and had no intention of studying there!

The next two years were at Naval Hospital St. Albans, LI, New York. There I learned more about the difference between Navy and civilian nursing. The Navy motto was to "Learn something well enough to teach it, teach it, then learn something else." Another was: "If it moves, salute it. If it does not move, pick it up. If you cannot pick it up, paint it!"

I worked on most units at the hospital, and then in pediatrics as assistant head nurse. On night duty, I was assigned to supervise many units. When assigned night duty, we were given two days off, worked twenty-eight nights, then were given two more days off. I loved New York City! At that time, if you were wearing your "dress uniform," you could get free tickets to Broadway plays, operas, and many other events in the city. I enjoyed parking my car outside of the city and walking through the different ethnic areas to browse through their stores, view their decors, and sample their foods.

However, I decided it was time for me to leave the Navy and return home. My last step before checking out was with a female Navy chief who convinced me to stay and request orders to Japan, assuring me that I could decline any orders sending me elsewhere. She also reminded me that there was no "draft" for women, meaning that women could leave the military at any time and not suffer being AWOL!

I was sent to San Francisco to board a ship headed to Japan in Sept., 1966. The twelve days aboard were wonderful! I watched in awe as whales nodded at us and dolphins raced along the side of the ship. When we arrived in Yokosuka, Japan, I asked the Navy to leave me there for the next twenty years. I absolutely loved it there, did much traveling, and met many friends. However, after one year, I had orders to Guam. The chief of nursing service enticed me to apply for a Regular Navy commission, which I did and was accepted.

Once in Guam, I had a fantastic time—except for Typhoon Karen that wiped out the second floor of Guam Memorial Hospital along with other destruction. As in Japan, I worked on most units, taught in the education department, and finally was assistant head nurse of OB and the nursery. There I delivered a few babies due to the doctor not arriving on time.

My next assignment was in September, 1963, to Great Lakes, IL, where I was eventually placed in charge of a new pediatric unit, and I loved it.

I was then asked to work in the education department where, within a week, all three of the senior nurses were gone due to illness, death in the family, and "STAT" orders to Vietnam. I was then *the* education department of one at the largest Naval hospitals in the U.S. at that time.

I had decided to go into missionary work and resign from the Navy. When I spoke with the director of the Nursing Department, she contacted the director of the Navy Nurse Corps in DC. She then asked me to join a seven-member Forward Surgical/Advisory Team to Vietnam. A Navy nurse friend from St. Albans, the only female on the team, and another friend, one of the surgeons on the team, asked me to join them. I eventually conceded and accepted orders to the team.

In Rach Gia, South Vietnam in 1966, I began my duty at a Vietnam

Provincial Hospital. We had no running water, no electricity, and only one generator—in the O.R. When not caring for U.S. troops, we provided surgical capabilities for Vietnamese and Cambodian military and citizens. I worked in pediatrics and post anesthesia, and post- op units. My friend Bev and I devised a distillery for the water we obtained from the many huge cement cisterns surrounding the hospital.

Eventually Bev and I established a clinic nearby to see the Vietnamese military dependents. They were not allowed to see our doctors or the Vietnamese military doctor, as they were not military. Nor could they see the hospital Vietnamese doctor, because they were not civilians. If Bev and I referred them with issues we could not handle, they could be seen by our surgeons or the only doctor at the hospital.

We traveled to outlying clinics, large, empty buildings where we could see, treat, or refer patients. Once I traveled with an advisor and his unit to a nearby island to administer immunization injections due to an outbreak of plague. While serving in Vietnam, I cared for and watched people as they died of horrific injuries, infections, in tetany and communicable diseases. I learned so much; some lessons were wonderful, others were not pleasant.

From Vietnam, I reported in March 1967 to the U.S. Naval Hospital in Quantico, VA, where I had the opportunity to care for Marines. Many of them were recovering from wounds and illnesses, etc. from Vietnam. I was in charge of the education department while being head nurse of pediatrics and then surgical units. The Navy was giving us many "hats" to wear!

Over time, the Navy had been asking me to be a recruiter. They suggested San Francisco, New York City, Ohio, and a few other areas, all of which I declined, stating that if/when Minneapolis was open, I would recruit there.

In early 1968, I received a call that Minneapolis was open. I was finally home! However, my area covered five states and I was out of the office most of the time.

My phone rang one day. The C.O. of the Navy ROTC at the University of Minnesota, a Navy captain, asked if I would attend a dinner at the university. Two Navy admirals were to be guest speakers. He asked me to come in my Mess Dress Uniform—frilly blouse, cumber bund, etc. At that time, very few people had seen women in uniform. He also asked me to bring an escort. I told him that I had no time to date. He laughed and said, "Just bring an escort!" After consulting my friend, a member of many Twin Cities Alumni Associations, we finally agreed on one man whom she would contact on my behalf.

Eventually, a gentleman named Vernon J. Bauer contacted me and agreed to be my escort. We dated each other for eighteen months before we were married!

When I left Vietnam in 1966, I was told to come home wearing civilian clothing and hide anything that would indicate that I was in the military, as we were targets for those protesting the Vietnam war. In Minneapolis as a Navy Nurse Recruiter, I was sometimes asked by male Navy recruiters to accompany them as they recruited at various universities and colleges. I stood beside them and told protesters that they were protesting the wrong people. I had just come from Vietnam and had lived with the Vietnamese. I told them exactly what was going on. And, if they wanted to protest, go to the state and federal capitols. Our Congress and the President are those who order war. We military personnel just do our jobs. We provided care for injured men and women who were American, Vietnamese, and Cambodian. My job in the military was to triage and treat whomever was injured, then transport them to the next best facility for their care. I wore my Navy uniform every day and at times drove home in a Navy car.

One morning in 1970, I was leaving for my office in downtown Minneapolis, which was a military recruiting station at that time (1960s-1970s), when I received a call from my C.O. He said not to report in, as my office, and one end of the Federal Office Building had just been blown up! Since the FBI was involved, the culprits were eventually discovered.

However, all over the nation, buildings that housed military recruiters and military personnel records were being targeted and destroyed. One of my brothers served in the Air Force and another in the Army during the 1950s. Their military records no longer exist, along with many others from that time and before. Many veterans who did not retain their DD 214—discharge records—are still fighting for help from the VA, as they attempt to resurrect papers that document their service.

Several months later, I was home with a friend when we heard a horrible explosion. My friend dashed outside, ignoring my shouts not to. She returned to say that the house next door was flattened like a pancake and was on fire! My husband, my friend, neighbors, police, and people from miles around thronged in our yard amid chards of fiery debris. Then my shoulder was tapped by a gentleman in a suit, white shirt, and tie. He asked if I was Commander (CDR) Bauer. I said, "Who is asking?" He and another like-attired gentleman flashed badges. They were with ONI (now called NCIS.) They advised me that the home next door had been demolished with plastic explosives purloined from the nearby New Brighton Arsenal and they believed the target had been me!

Thus, I was requested to sell my home, no longer wear my uniform, or drive a Navy vehicle to my home. My neighbors, who lived in the home next door, died in the explosion.

***

Vern and I wanted children, however my time to conceive had passed. We attempted to adopt. The Navy said I should remain in MN on recruiting duty until an adoption was completed. However, the adoption agencies would not accept our application while I was on active duty. Also, we were considered at ages thirty-three and thirty-five to be too old to adopt. The alternative was to resign my regular commission and accept a reserve commission. I very reluctantly did that.

Still wanting children, I was placed on massive doses of Premarin by my OB/GYN; however, the drug was so potent that I just quit taking it. While at work one afternoon in 1972, I received a call from the adoption agency—they had a baby for us! I was so excited that I forgot to ask if the baby was male or female! We adopted our Jeff as soon as the agency would allow—three months later.

Several months after adopting our Jeff, I awoke one morning and told my husband that I was pregnant. He was skeptical and said I should call the doctor, who was also skeptical and suggested that I come in for an exam. It seems the Premarin had done its duty!

I gave birth to our son, Terry, in May, 1973.

***

I worked in ICU at Miller Hospital, which merged with St. Luke's, and eventually became United Hospital in the Allina Corporation. I taught Emergency Medical Education at United and all Allina Hospitals and Clinics in the Twin Cities and surrounding areas. I was encouraged by one of my sisters to start a First Aid and a CPR one-credit course at one of the largest technical colleges in the state. I had been teaching CPR as a volunteer at inner city churches and day care centers, women's shelters, and family-owned resorts in northern MN for many years. I then developed a course and taught at three technical colleges.

Since I was still in the Navy Reserves and was required to be on duty every other weekend, as well as going on active duty at least two weeks every year, I could not accept full-time work or supervision at the hospital.

Between 1974 to 1993, I served on A.T in Naval hospitals in San Diego; Great Lakes; Key West; Bremerton; Hameln, Germany; England; Washington, D.C.; Marine Corps Headquarters, VA; Office of the Director of the Navy Nurse Corps in D.C.; Nashville; San Antonio; New Orleans; and many other areas.

I remained in the Navy Reserves for twenty-two years and had completed thirty-five years in the Navy. I had joined in September of 1958 and resigned in September of 1993.

In 1984 I was contacted by Diane Evans. She asked me to join with six women who had served as nurses in Vietnam. Diane's mission was to place a Vietnam Nurse Memorial in Washington, D.C. On Nov. 11, 1993, we were all with Diane as she accomplished that with the dedication of the Vietnam Women's Memorial near the Vietnam Wall!

We also worked with the Minneapolis VA to develop women's programs. This was a very long struggle which continues. However, the Minneapolis VAMC is now rated top in the nation and has many women-oriented programs and services.

***

I would not have remained in the Navy for thirty-five years if I did not enjoy it. The friends I made there are still best friends. Yet, the military remains a "man's world." The struggles for us women persist with the "invisibility factor." I have spoken to men about their service, only to have them address my husband instead of me when they responded! When seeing my Vietnam license plates and/or my shirts or car stickers, both men and other women have said to me, "Please thank your husband for his service." When wearing a cap or hat with a Navy or Vietnam logo, I have also been asked to please thank my husband for his service. Rarely have I been asked, "Where did you serve?" And rarely has someone said to me, "Thank you for your service."

My message for other American women is that which my mother always said to me: "Do whatever you think is best for you." You can accomplish whatever you want, whenever you want. Just continue to work for it. God bless you and keep you in His/Her loving arms!

SEVEN

Holly Breeden

Spc. Holly Breeden, E-4
WI National Guard, 2002-2014

*U*NTIL SIXTH GRADE, I resided in Superior, WI. Then my family made a decision to move to Webster, WI, where I spent the remainder of my middle school and high school years.

It was in the sixth grade that I met Amber. We became inseparable from the start. In high school, I was very active in sports and activities. I had seen others in my family make poor decisions at young ages, and I wanted a different path. Keeping myself busy kept me out of trouble. Amber and I were always there for each other, through thick and thin. She had a rough childhood and her family relationships were strained. She got good grades until we were in the tenth grade. Amber started spending time with others who encouraged bad habits and she was making poor decisions herself. I tried to warn her, but she was beginning a downward spiral, and didn't want to listen to anyone, including me.

We were in the school library on September 11, 2001 when the television stunned everyone with continual coverage of the attack on the Twin Towers in New York City. A few weeks later, our school was visited by recruiters from every branch of the military. Amber and I listened to all of them. We were seventeen years old and neither of us knew what we would do after graduation. College was out of reach for both of us because our families could not pay for it.

We really wanted to help our country to defend against terrorism and if we could do that while positioning ourselves for our futures, it seemed like a no-brainer. My two grandfathers, uncle, and my dad served in the military, and I wanted to make him proud. Amber and I were most impressed with the recruiter from the WI National Guard. He said if we enlisted, the Guard would let us remain in high school until called upon, and best of all—they would pay for our college tuition. At seventeen, Amber and I enlisted in the WI National guard under the Buddy System on June 18, 2002.

My dad, who is an Army vet, was proud of my decision, but hesitant because he had seen how women were treated in the service. My Uncle Gene was proud too, and my friends were happy for me. I was happy with the prospect of getting Amber away from those who were a bad influence on her. Throughout our senior year, she and I periodically reported for drills with the 724 Engineer Battalion out of Superior, WI. We graduated in June 2003.

Two weeks later, Amber and I were on our way to Fort Jackson, SC, for basic training. We had been warned that there would be lots of yelling by drill sergeants, and they were right! It seemed like they didn't know how to talk—just YELL!

I was very competitive at Basic when it came to the athletic portion. On the Army Physical Fitness Exam, I scored a 389, landing me on the "extended scale." I completed ninety-six sit-ups, ninety-two push-ups, and ran a 13:19 two-mile run. I was awarded a three-star general coin. I was the Battalion Guideon, which was an honor.

The military did wonders for my friend. We both were assigned to be squad leaders and we enjoyed that. Amber was forced to work out, run obstacle courses, and learn how to fire weapons. She was forced to abandon any bad habits as the military applied their "break you down, then build you back up" system. It was great to have my best friend back again, and going through Basic together made it all easier.

During Advanced Individual Training (AIT) we were both designated Light Weight Diesel Mechanics based on our ASVAB scores. We worked on all parts of military vehicles.

We were able to get weekend passes, which we mostly spent chilling out.

I had to complete a y2 designator course that changed my job from a light-wheeled vehicle mechanic to a heavy-wheeled vehicle mechanic, which included working on tanks.

Amber was already out at that point. By September 2005, Amber had a husband, two children, and was pregnant. It was difficult to separate from her, but I understood that her family needed her, and she had to leave the military.

In early 2010, I received orders to deploy. However, I injured my back when I slipped and fell on a wet clay hill while doing a training exercise at Camp Blanding, FL. I had gone through all of the medical exams prior to this and was ready to go. I was so upset because I wanted to deploy, but I did not have the chance to do so. I was "refraded" (temporary medical release from active duty) and sent to home station because of the injury.

Two weeks after I was home, I learned that I was pregnant. This was something that I did not believe due to the fact that I was previously told by a doctor that I was not able to have children. Amber was one of the first to know. She had just had her baby girl. She went with me to the doctor and it was confirmed that I was indeed pregnant. I gave birth to a healthy baby girl in December 2010, and another in November 2012.

I left the National Guard in 2014 due to the back injury that had occurred in 2010 since it had not gotten better, but it was hard to leave. The military becomes an extended family.

It took so long for the MEB/PEB process as they lost my paperwork four times! I am now 30% disabled.

***

I am proud that I served, but at times I feel forgotten—"invisible." Even though I did not deploy, I am still important. It took me a while to say that because I was so upset that I did not get to go with my unit; my family.

I am now the Chapter Captain in Duluth, MN, for "Team RWB" (Red, White, Blue), an organization whose mission is to "enrich the lives of America's veterans by connecting them to their community through physical and social activity."

Amber and I are still best friends.

My message for other American women is this: Be bold, take chances, volunteer, don't put up with the bullshit, be strong, love yourself. Believe in yourself.

EIGHT

Victoria Citrowske

Captain Victoria Citrowske
US Air Force, 2000-2007

G ROWING UP ON a hobby farm, I learned the value of hard work and service from a young age. There was always much work to accomplish when living on ten acres, where my family did some sharecropping of corn and alfalfa with our neighbors. We raised chickens, goats, and ducks. My older sister, my twin brother, and I were kept busy with chores each day. While others our age perhaps were playing video games and watching cartoons, we were hauling firewood around and tending to our animals. Little did I know that these chores and small sacrifices were readying me for my time in the "blue suit."

My world was turned upside down when my parents divorced when I was nine years old. However, it was for the best and groomed me to be an independent individual. Four years later, my mom, twin brother, and I moved from the farm to a new house in Apple Valley, MN. My drive and determination served me well in my new environment. I excelled in several sports in high school, as a five-sport varsity athlete, to include: ringette, hockey (Captain—junior and senior year), cross-country running (Captain—senior year,) soccer and track (Captain—senior year). I served as Captain of the first ever Girls State High School Hockey team, which provided us the honor of a place in the Hockey Hall of Fame. Other in-school and out-of-school activities kept me incredibly busy and "well-rounded," and academics never took a back seat to sports.

After playing five sports in high school at the varsity level and being a state champion in three of them, as well as earning academic achievements, the time had come for me to decide what was next for me. After visiting the Air Force Academy in 8th grade, I was certain I'd spend my college years there. It seemed more than just a pipe dream. I also felt I was destined to be in the military, despite never wanting to be like everyone else. I desired to be a leader, make a difference, and fly into the blue yonder, but my lack of height hindered the third goal. Little did I know that my desire to attend a service academy entailed such a long, harrowing process to apply, obtain a nomination, and then receive an appointment.

As part of the decision-making process, while attacking the arduous task of applying to the academies, I visited both the Air Force Academy and West Point on athletic recruiting trips. It was incredibly tough to decide which path I should take: Air Force Academy, West Point or Marine NROTC scholarship. I ultimately chose the Air Force Academy, as it had been my "pipe dream." I felt it was where I belonged and I also had a feeling that the Air Force was the most accepting of sisters into the brotherhood of arms.

Neither my dad, who had served as an Army enlisted infantryman in Vietnam, nor my stepgrandfather, who had served as a top turret gunner on a B-26 during WWII (a man who survived time as a POW in Germany for three months during WWII), shared much about their time in uniform. While no fault of either of these men, admittedly so, I knew very little of what I was about to embark upon, both at the U.S. Air Force Academy and in the active duty Air Force.

In the summer of 1996, I reported to the U.S. Air Force Academy in Colorado Springs, CO, for six weeks of Basic Cadet Training. Unlike most entering USAFA, I had the good fortune of having my twin brother also starting the Academy "adventure" alongside me. I knew I was in for a whole host of things that would change, shape, and challenge me in the days, months, and years ahead when a cadre member jumped on our bus and said, "Basics! You have ten seconds to get off this bus, and you've already wasted nine!" The first three weeks of Basic Training were held at the USAFA campus, known as "the hill." These weeks were spent primarily on indoctrination, learning the fundamentals and expectations for USAFA cadets, as well as principles of the Air Force—taking us from civilian young adults to basic cadets in an incredibly brief timeframe.

The second three weeks of basic were held at "Jack's Valley"—a site on the Academy grounds, which was similar to a M*A*S*H-like set-up. The focus shifted more to physical training.

We were challenged with several "courses": some using and building our warrior minds and ethos, while all the time pushing us to and beyond our physical limits. During this time, I recall many formation runs in full BDUs (battle dress uniform) and boots, carrying our rubber rifle (M-16 without a firing pin and a lead muzzle), affectionately known as "rifle runs." After surviving these life-changing six weeks, we were ready to become first-year cadets (known as "Doolies") at the end of Basic Training in mid-August 1996.

During the summer after my Doolie year, I completed parachute training (Jump School) at USAFA, and I earned my parachute wings. Later that summer at the Academy, I endured Combat Survival Training (CST), furthering my resolve to become an officer in the Air Force.

There was a plethora of opportunities that came my way at USFAFA, which furthered my character and passion for helping others. The most notable of these were my two instances in serving as Basic Training cadre. The summer heading into my junior year, I served as cadre during second Basic Training, in a Flight Specialist role. In this role, I was cadre member, but also a peer counselor to a flight of thirty basic cadets. The summer heading into my senior year, I served as cadre during first basic training, in a Flight Specialist ACIC (Assistant Cadet In Charge) role. In this role, I managed the forty flight specialists and did a lot of heavy lifting with some basic cadet behaviorally/emotionally-charged situations.

The four years at the Academy were some of the toughest times I had and have ever experienced. Juggling the incredibly challenging, heavy engineering course load, meeting military expectations, and performing as a Division I athlete in two sports (soccer and track) was more than one could handle. But, that was the point of USAFA—pushing cadets to go beyond their limits, and succeed while doing so. Despite seemingly having to move mountains in order to graduate, I wouldn't change my decision to attend USAFA, as the bonds created and experiences had were things that perhaps aren't tangible, but remain some of my most valued "things."

**

As I was too short to fly, I selected a career field that correlated to my field of study in college. I was elated to be one of five earning a Behavioral Scientist slot from my class of 1,000 cadets. I walked into USAFA with next to nothing as a naïve civilian, and left with gold bars on my shoulders and a strong sense of character, integrity, and excitement for my opportunity to excel in service to our country. I also could say that I got a "BS in BS," earning a Bachelor of Science degree in Behavioral Sciences.

I served in the active duty Air Force from 2000 to 2007 in various roles as a Behavioral Scientist, briefly involving development and analysis of attitude and opinion surveys for the Air Force, but primarily involving Enlisted Promotion Test Development—writing exams, editing exams, and managing the pagination, printing, shipping, scoring, and reporting of all Air Force Enlisted Specialty Knowledge Tests. During this time, I was also fortunate enough to obtain a Master of Arts degree in Industrial/Organizational Psychology.

The front and end caps of my military career were special duty assignments. I began my career back in Minnesota, as a recruiter for the high school population for the Air Force Academy and AFROTC, and I ended my career as an AFROTC instructor at UCLA, teaching two academic classes per term, serving as an academic advisor for the cadets, recruiting for our detachment, and participating in the physical and military training of the cadets at the UCLA. Before exiting the Air Force, I completed Squadron Officer School (SOS) in the fall of 2006, initially begrudgingly. While at SOS, I won the "Fleet Feet" Award for the female with the fastest three-mile in our class of approximately five hundred individuals.

***

In the fall of 2007, it was time for me to step away from military service and reconnect with my family back home in Minnesota. It was bittersweet leaving the Air Force, and bitter cold to move back to the chilly North. It has been some time since I wore my Air Force blues, and I honestly have missed the military camaraderie.

I also wanted to give back in the ways I experienced, from the time in which I was applying to USAFA, to the day when our hats were thrown in the air, with the Air Force Thunderbirds doing a flyby overhead. In January 2018, I became a USAF Academy Admissions Liaison Officer (ALO), where I volunteer, providing assistance to prospective cadets throughout the application and admission process, as well as during their time at USAFA. I also participate in congressional interviews for candidates seeking nominations to the four service academies. In doing these things, I feel I have a stake in selecting our future leaders of America.

I greatly appreciate and value the opportunities I was afforded while in the military. The tools bestowed upon me while in the Air Force have remained long after I shed the blue suit. The military mentality is never far from my mind, and remains part of who I am today. There are three things from my time at USAFA that perpetually echo in my mind: "Perception is reality," "How you look is how you are," and "You are always on parade."

Despite being far from the battlefield during my military career, I still am proud of my service to our country. I've been a part of something that I share with my twin brother, a current Air Force Reservist, my stepdad as a former F-4 pilot in Vietnam, my dad as a former infantryman in Vietnam, and my stepgrandfather as a former B-26 top turret gunner in WWII.

Thankfully, women in the service are becoming more visible and accepted, by way of the increasing percentages of women in the service, the progression of our military, as well as the advancement of society. Minnesota recently created a license plate specifically for female veterans, and I'm proud to display my "Woman Veteran" plates. Women are crucial to the strength of our military, and we are not "invisible."

***

As a female in a male-dominated military subculture, it wasn't always easy, at the Air Force Academy or in the active duty Air Force. Nevertheless, it only increased my drive to pursue success. I encourage any females interested in serving to take the step we all did to serve our country. The more of us that serve, the more visible the female soldiers are in the military and in the country in which we represent.

NINE

LaTia DeAmparo

Sergeant LaTia DeAmparo
US Army, 1984-86, USAR, 1988-91

I AM OF CUBAN Senegalese, (Father) Native American Choctaw, Irish and English (Mother) decent. I was born in 1965 and raised in the great neighborhood of Hyde Park, Chicago, IL. Our family functioned like a village. They owned a two-flat home on Drexel Avenue and I had the luxury of being raised by both parents and grandparents. Several extended family members also lived nearby and I was blessed to be raised around them. Our neighborhood was enriched with astute African American families that consisted of spiritual folk, business owners, musicians, and lovers of the arts.

My parents divorced when I was an infant and my mother built several businesses to maintain our family. She remarried, and together with my stepfather owned and operated three businesses on the south side of Chicago. My stepfather was a self-made business man with a twelfth-grade education. He was respected and knew the ways of the world. My mother was formally educated and received her Bachelors Degree in Business from George Williams College, formally known as Chicago YMCA College on Drexel. She came from a long line of family-owned businesses and managed all of the operations while also working a full-time job for the federal government. My grandparents were members of Chicago's R. Nathaniel Dett Club of Music and Allied Arts, which is one of the oldest active branches of the National Association of Negro Musicians (NANM). They traveled all over the world and their legacy of music is recorded in the Center for Black Music Research Library and Archives. They made sure I wanted for nothing, and I loved and admired them with all of my heart.

As my parents built a family business, my grandparents built my foundation. They were tasked to ensure that I become knowledgeable of the presence of God, and to recognize my abilities and to stay in gratitude for what I had in life. They also understood the world and provided a strong foundation that was filled with discipline and grace. "To thine own self be true" was spoken often in our home. I am so very blessed to have received this early on in life. They always encouraged me to follow my own path through creativity and culture. They ensured that I studied classical piano, voice, and modeling. By the age of six, I was performing in theatre productions of Handel's "Messiah" and by my freshman year at Lindblom HS, I'd become a featured vocalist and pianist. My talents lead me to local talent shows and pageants and by 1982, I became Miss Illinois Prince Hall Masonic jurisdiction, winning a scholarship for college.

During elementary school I realized early on that I was different. I was mocked and shamed for my beauty, ethnicity, cultural up-bringing, and intelligence as others could not simply define me, so they attempted to defame me. Thank goodness I had a large enough family to keep them at bay. My hair was long, brown, and wavy with blonde and red highlights; my face was round and dotted with small moles and freckles; and my completion was very light. The biggest debate on the playground would always be, "So what is she?" It took countless after-school fights to prove what I wasn't! And sure as hell I was not going to be bullied, mistreated, or teased. In our house, Momma had one rule: "They can talk all they want, but Baby, if they put their hands on you, then give them what they asked for!"

Day in and out, I was challenged. I was not black enough for the black girls, not white enough for the white girls, not Spanish "at all," and heaven forbid I be considered the girl with the "good Indian hair." One person told me that I didn't look like the Spanish people he knew so I couldn't possibly be Spanish. This rhetoric was ridiculous, and quite naturally I became despondent of ignorant people. I withdrew from outsiders and just went through the motions to get school finished as soon as possible. I did my own thing and found myself gravitating to others who were much like myself. The children were bad, but some of the teachers were worse. Folks would even mispronounce my name as if it was a bother to learn, so they would just make up one that was close and easier to digest because it was not the social norm. I just gave up correcting them as they would regress and take offense.

I was no longer sheltered by my family and the outside world had so many different views and definitions of who I was, it became a constant struggle for me to correct them and tell them *Who I Am*! And so as my world became wider, I began to develop my own sense of self and I believe *that* is where my tolerance for ignorance came to an end and I began to have a passion for law and equality. I realized the world was unjust and unfair. I found myself constantly defending my right to be who I am, so why not further my career as a lawyer? The issue was I hated school and really wanted to travel to other countries, much like my grandparents, and experience this rich, diverse world I'd seen and heard about as a child.

My best friend was a kind energetic soul. She was looking for a way out too. She encouraged me to enlist in the Army with her on the buddy system's delayed entry program and assured me that was our ticket to Germany.

Most of my childhood friends thought I was just crazy. I thought they were too because they were having babies, with no jobs, getting high and going to the same lakefront parties and bars. What a waste of time. My family supported my decision as they knew I had to do something: Go to college, get a job, or move on my own.

After meeting the recruiter, I took the ASVAB test and was enrolled for AIT (Advanced Individual Training) as a law clerk. My mother signed the paperwork and I was enlisted into the US Army at the age of seventeen under the delayed entry program with my best friend on the buddy system.

Upon reporting to MEPS (Military Entrance Processing Stations), I weighed in two pounds overweight and was forced to stay back two weeks until I made the required weight. When I returned, the processor told me that my MOS (Military Occupational Specialty) was no longer available and I had to be a MP (Military Police) instead. This was yet another incident that changed my life compass. I proceeded to basic training at Ft. McClellan, AL, and in 1984 I was deployed to Frankfurt, Germany, with the Gibbs Kaserne Military 709th Battalion, V Corp, 82nd Airborne Division.

I can never forget my first assignment as I witnessed a soldier's severed remains lying across the Hauptbahnhof tracks during a rain storm. My first job as a private was to set up a traffic control point near the body and direct traffic until the US Medic Corps arrived. What a welcome! Life in a G-Unit-MP Garrison Unit required that you were squared away and elite, as we were always in the public eye. At times you would never know when or where you could be assigned.

Military housing, domestic, transport assignments, motor pool, honor guard, crowd control, railways, air convoys, drug force, and K-9 medical assistance were all part of the job.

During my personal time, I reconnected with my childhood buddy. We traveled and partied all throughout Europe and eventually I managed to fall in love with a wonderful engineer who was stationed miles away in Darmstadt, Germany. Keeping to my musical roots, I performed as a vocalist in the VCorps VSO tours. I also enjoyed my volunteer work as the assistant coach of a young boys' basketball team with my NCOIC.

My NCOIC (Non-Commissioned Officer in Charge) and I worked very closely in the field and with the basketball team. He found me attractive but was made aware that I was dating someone else. One day he made mention of a date during a GI party (clean up detail). He was persistent, and I was rude to him when I refused. I look back on that now and think that it was very embarrassing for him. This embarrassment and rejection soon led to harassment as he would eavesdrop on my phone conversations at the hall desk and make smart remarks about me in public. The more I rejected him the worse thing got. Eventually I stopped coaching the ball team to avoid him. So he used his rank to have me in his presence and to continue annoying me.

One day he assigned me to an extra cleaning detail and I told him out right, "Fuck you!" He replied, "That's disrespect to an NCO, DeAmparo" and I replied, "Yep, Fuck you, Sergeant!" and proceeded to go to my room and lock the door. As a CQ, he had keys to all rooms in the barracks. He followed behind me. I heard the keys rattling as he unlocked my door and that's when I fully engaged him with my baton. I struck him in the throat, face and knees. Once he reached the floor, I repeatedly whaled him in the head.

Two other members of the squad dragged him out and all I can remember was his screaming, "This shit ain't over, DeAmparo! I'm gonna write your black ass up, believe that!" His screams rang through the barracks, but in an instant you could have heard a pin drop as doors opened and then shut amongst us. The hallways were empty yet everyone in the barracks knew what just happened; our squad operated with a blind eye including myself because assaults can never take place in a MP battalion. No one came to my defense—because I defended my damn self! It was like the playground all over again. He kept taunting me so I gave him what he asked for without regrets. I cried in anger, rationalized, felt remorse, and then quickly shook off that feeling as I tossed back a few shots of scotch. All of a sudden, I reset back to duty. I pressed out my uniform and soft buffed my boots; it was imperative that I stand tall to face judgement for my actions.

Three knocks at the door and I was escorted down to the company commander. He was young and astute. I explained my harassment case. "He liked me, I rejected him, and he would not let up," I told him. The commander listened quietly as he wrote some notes on his pad and turned to me and asked, "Do you want to stay here soldier?" I replied, "There's no way I'm gonna make it here anymore, Sir, I won't survive." To this day, I believe he felt the very same way.

I was issued an Article 15, reduced in rank from a specialist to a private, and relieved from duty. All of my personal weapons were stored for shipment and I was no longer able to wear an authorized weapon of any kind. I felt anguished and disgusted.

I was placed on motor pool duty and isolated during my last two weeks. Formally my DD214 (Discharge from Active Duty form) reads "Honorable Discharge," and in the comments below it states "Unsatisfactory Performance." What a huge contradiction! I left the service in 1986. But in retrospect I thank the commander for trying to do half-way right by me, and his decision actually gave me a second military chance in the Army Reserves.

I went directly into the Minnesota Army Reserves, where they changed my MOS to Psychological Operations, and I regained my rank. I also gained a secondary MOS of Administrative Specialist as an E-5 SGT and had a wonderful experience for four years under the 349th PSYOP at Fort Snelling, MN.

I chose not to be a victim or be defined by my DD214. Personally, being labeled "unsatisfactory" only confirmed my beliefs from childhood and motivated me to fight even harder. I've always been passionate about equity and fair treatment because I've experienced and witnessed discrimination in one form or another for decades.

It took me a while to complete this memoir because I began to get agitated every time I went to the tablet. Subconsciously I've suppressed this crap for over thirty-six years. Writing has helped me to unlock the anxiety.

I reached out to the VA Women's Clinic and my primary physician diagnosed me with PTSD. Mental Health Services are scheduled next week and now I am on a new journey to recovery.

***

Since leaving the military, I have worked in numerous community programs advocating equal employment, homeless veteran re-integration, and mediation and development training.

My entire career now is dedicated to work in law: equal rights, compliance, pay equity, women veteran resources, affirmative action, and diversity and inclusion.

I currently work with the Disabled Veteran Outreach Program (DVOP) for Women Veterans, which provides job search guidance and strategies as well as training. I have served as Employment/Case Manager for the MN Assistance Council for Veterans, and partnered with MN DEED to launch the Homeless Veteran Re-integration Program (HVRP). I served with the MN Dept. of Human Rights as a Senior Compliance Officer and Equal Pay Team Leader, and as EEO Officer and Manager at Metropolitan State University in the Twin Cities, MN.

My view as an EEO Officer is that often times people misuse their sense of responsibilities (authorities) in the workplace consciously and/or unconsciously. Discrimination is rooted in ignorance and fear and can be fueled by an individual's personal bias, learned behavior, or world experiences. The EEO Officer is charged with the duty to make sure this does not occur in either employment practices or by employees.

We actually look at things in a reverse context in order to find the possible violations to the law. For example, the EEO officer also advises the employer on how to be prepared to address those situations with skilled training, HR professionals, and managers to prevent violations.

The Office of Equal Opportunity (OEO) is responsible for the set of laws and policies that mandate all individuals' rights to equal opportunity irrespective of race, religion, color, gender, sexual orientation, national origin, age, disability or genetic information.

Professionally, I've grown and embraced equal employment with several organizations. Do I see a future of equity, diversity, and inclusion in our military? Time brings about change. Our US military has evolved and is by far the most diverse organization in the world. But unlike any organization, the military is "armed forces responsible for securing and defending our country." It is designed for war, and it will never be perfect or without unspoken injustices, as war and conflict never have a perfect resolution.

For years, I did not acknowledge myself as a veteran. Now I am the spokeswoman for the Women Veterans Initiative of Minnesota.

My message to other women veterans who have or are feeling a veil of "invisibility" regarding their military service is this: Time brings about change, and I encourage every woman to speak up for herself and let the world know that she is not invisible!

My prayer is for a world where we love one another, show compassion and mutual respect by allowing people the right to just "be!" That we awaken and address our fear of learning how to love one another for humanity's sake.

I love and trust myself enough to know that I must continue to stay in faith, to live in the present, address my fears, and encourage others to speak their truth. As you read my story, I can only pray that it reaches others and encourages them to "Stay Empowered, Stay Beautiful, Stay Visible!"

Always,

Your Sister Soldier,

LaTia

TEN

Jennifer Diaz

Chief Warrant Officer 3 Jennifer Diaz
US Army National Guard, MNARNG, 1995-2019

MY CHILDHOOD WAS fairly typical—actually it was great. On November 25, 1975, I was born in St. Paul, MN, and raised in the town of Cottage Grove. Dad worked full time and my mom stayed home with me and my younger brother. We would make forts, ride bikes, and play in the park. We didn't take a lot of vacations, but we did make a few trips to visit family in Texas, and once we went to the Wisconsin Dells when I was five or six years old. When I got to be a teenager, I would run around with my friends outside in the summer all day, having a great time.

My mom opened a ceramic shop in South St. Paul. After a few years of owning that shop, she decided she wanted to be home more and she moved her business to our house. I remember all the ladies coming throughout the week on "their days" for classes. They always had a good time and there was lots of laughter.

While growing up, I played soccer, and when I attended Park High School, although I was nowhere near being a star athlete, I had a blast and enjoyed being part of the team. I ran track as well in the spring. I enjoyed being part of the Theater Club and participated in a few plays in high school and college. I always enjoyed music and I played piano, alto saxophone, flute, piccolo, and took voice lessons. I started working at McDonalds in Cottage Grove and worked there for seven and a half years during high school and afterward.

Following my graduation from Park High, I went on to college at Southwest State (now Minnesota State University-Southwest) until 1997 and majored in Broadcast Journalism. Ever since I was five years old, my dream job was to be a news anchor on KSTP, Channel 5 TV, in St. Paul. Unfortunately, I was unable to finish my last year of college at the time due to finances.

As a teenager, I had never considered joining the military and I remember telling the recruiters who called that I would never join, so please stop calling. Then one day I was listening to the radio and heard the commercial for the Army Reserves.

I thought that I could do one weekend a month and two weeks in the summer. I figured I might try it.

Meanwhile, I got a job working in a TCF bank out of the West St. Paul Cub Foods and the Cottage Grove location needed a fill-in for a few days, so I volunteered. One day a guy came to my bank window in an Army uniform and I simply told him I wanted to enlist in the Army and asked him how I could join. He asked how long I had been thinking about it. I told him "a few days." I gave him my phone number and told him to have his recruiter call me the next day because I wanted to join the Army.

I hadn't talked to any other branches. The next day the Army recruiter called me and we went through the process. I originally went to MEPS (Military Entrance Processing Station) and was disqualified due to having bunions. I needed a waiver, but right after the waiver was submitted, the government shut down, so I was delayed in enlisting and had to wait from

October to December 5, 1995 to sign up at the age of twenty. I actually ended up joining the MN Army National Guard. I just thought it sounded like it might be fun, and I thought I could help preserve what our forefathers fought for.

I think both of my parents were shocked. I believe they never thought it would be something I would be interested in. My mom worried more than my dad and still does to this day, but she knows how much I love it. They were extremely supportive and still are. My dad and grandfathers were both Navy men, so my dad has always joked with me that I am a traitor, but he's proud of my service. My brother has always supported me. My friends were surprised at first, but again, they too supported me through it.

I was sent to Basic Training in January 1996 and Advanced Individual Training in March of that same year, and both were at Fort Jackson, SC.

Throughout both experiences I just went along with everything they threw at us. While it was difficult, I really enjoyed the routine of everything. I also thought that it was great because we got paid for everything we did.

I got teased by our company's First Sergeant because I was so skinny. He would tease me during our marksmanship training, asking me how I held myself up with my arms because they were so skinny. I just laughed. (He wasn't lying. I still have skinny arms!)

One day I was in the fastest running group with all men and the Company Commander decided to run with that group. He happened to be running by me. We had our sweatshirt hoods up and we were calling cadence when he shouted loudly, "You all need to sound off! You sound like a bunch of girls!" I looked over at him and he looked at me and said, "Oh, that's because you are a girl!" I replied, "I sure am and I don't want to sound like a boy…I like sounding like a girl!" and I continued my run.

I was assigned as a Unit Clerk, Personnelist (Human Resources NCO is the official name). I was in charge of Non-Commissioned Officer Enlisted Review: NCOERS (ensuring they were completed, completed on time, and submitted for filing). Officer Evaluation Reports, or OERs, are the same as the enlisted evaluations. I reviewed, submitted, and tracked awards; reviewed, and tracked enlisted officer promotions; and updated all mandatory forms (life insurance, housing allowance, direct deposit, updated enlisted record briefs and officer record briefs.) It was the perfect position for me, and I was both pleased and proud of my contribution to our Army National Guard.

On 23 September 2018 I will be deploying to Kuwait as the Sexual Assault Response Coordinator for the 34th Infantry Division, and I will manage the program and sexual assault response for approximately 10,000 soldiers. I will be stationed at Camp Arifjan, Kuwait, for an expected nine to ten months, and I am looking forward to my deployment. I believe it will be a great experience and a real adventure.

***

I eventually completed my four-year degree (it took seventeen years, but I finished in 2011), and went on to get my Masters Degree in Forensic Psychology.

My husband and I have three sons, Roman, Maximilian, and Reagan, and a daughter, Claire, who will be in the care of their dad and close family members throughout my deployment.

I will have twenty-three years of experience in the MN National Guard in December, 2018. I still enjoy serving, so I will stay until it is no longer enjoyable.

I have truly enjoyed my time in the military. I think as a female there has been discrimination to deal with over the years. I feel like I have had to work harder to be taken seriously and to have people realize that I was guiding them and advising them correctly. I have faced a lot of sexual harassment over the years. I don't think at the time that I realized some of it was sexual harassment, but looking back, it certainly was. Those behaviors and comments are not geared toward the males, but somehow, when directed toward a female, it seemed to be ok.

There are times as well that I felt like less of a soldier because I hadn't been deployed yet. I know that I am not less, and my career has mostly been wonderful. I have accomplished so much and done a lot of good for the organization, but there were times that not having the deployment experience has made me feel not as significant—in other words, "invisible." After talking with other people, I have now learned to recognize that I am a veteran, and with my upcoming deployment, it will no longer be an issue for me. Still, I mostly get overlooked in public, especially when I am with my husband. People will always assume that he is in the service or a vet. He is asked about his service or for his Military ID in order to get a discount. He is so supportive and politely corrects them, saying that they need to ask me.

It's disheartening that I still have to correct almost everyone, but it's necessary so the military service of women is not "invisible" and that people know that "We serve as well."

My statement to other American women is this: Do whatever you want to do. Go after your goals and dreams because you deserve them. You can accomplish anything that you set your mind to. Don't be afraid to try things and experience things. Everything is a learning and growing experience. You have so much potential and there are always people to support you and help you.

ELEVEN

Patsy Steiner-Dillon

Commander Patsy Steiner-Dillon (Ret.)
US Navy, 1976-2017

I WAS RAISED on a dairy and beef farm in western Wisconsin in a large family of six girls and three boys. I was number six. Although I like the rural environment, farming (i.e. milking cows and bailing hay in ninety-degree weather with high humidity) was not for me. I decided at an early age that I wanted something different for myself.

During my senior year of high school, I was looking for a pathway to many possibilities and opportunities. I had to find a job! After talking with my older sister, Linda, it seemed that the Navy could be a good place for me. The economy was not very good in 1976/1977. My sister Linda really encouraged me to join the Navy because she had wanted to join herself; however, her decision was diverted for another reason…she met her husband. I owe Linda a great deal for encouraging me to join the Navy. I did not consider any of the other branches.

Still, I asked my dad if I should join the Navy. He said it was my decision. I was shocked with his response, since I always had to ask if I could go out on a Saturday night, but now when I really wanted his opinion, he opted not to tell me. His rationalization was sound advice, looking back at it now. He said, "If I tell you to go and you hate it, then you will blame me. If I tell you not to go, and you end up regretting not going, then you will blame me. So, this is your decision." He was a very wise man!

I enlisted at the age of eighteen on December 30, 1976 under the Naval Reserve Delayed Entry Program. On September 30, 1977, I left for Recruit Training Center (boot camp), Orlando, FL.

Following boot camp, I attended Aviation Administration (AZ) "A" School in Meridian, MS, where I graduated #1 in my class. I was assigned to Carrier Airborne Early Warning Training Squadron One Ten at Naval Air Station Miramar, San Diego, CA, from March 1978-1981.

Following my tour in San Diego, I attended Data Analysis "C" School, graduating #2 in my class. After graduation, I transferred to the Aircraft Intermediate Department, Naval Station, Rota, Spain.

I left active service in December 1981, and in May 1982, I joined the Naval Reserve and was immediately advanced to Petty Officer First Class while assigned to Fighter Squadron Composite 13 at Naval Air Station Miramar, San Diego, CA. After a couple of years, I transferred to Patrol Squadron Ninety-One at Naval Air Station Moffett Field, CA, in 1984, along with my husband, who was an active duty Sailor.

In 1985, I began a new tour with Patrol Squadron Sixty at Naval Air Station Glenview, IL. I loved this squadron! It is a highlight of my naval career. I was promoted to Chief Petty Officer and was promoted to Ensign as a commissioned officer in 1988 and 1990, respectively.

After my commissioning, I transferred to the Naval Air Reserve Center, Minneapolis, MN, serving in aviation units until my acceptance and transfer into the Naval Reserve Intelligence Program in 1994. Upon completion of my intelligence training in 1995, I was assigned to Joint Intelligence Center Pacific 0178 as an intelligence analyst and then as the Deputy for Awards for Reserve Intelligence for our region.

After a long tour with Joint Intelligence Center Pacific 0178, I transferred to Commander, Naval Forces Japan Headquarters in Minneapolis for two years, then transferred to Commander, United States Forces Joint Command in Akron, Ohio.

In November, 2010, I was selected and appointed as the Executive Officer of the United States European Command 0289, Minneapolis, MN prior to my mobilization in August 2011.

My *real* deployment was my tour in support of Operation Enduring Freedom, Kabul, Afghanistan, from August 2011 until August 2012. I was fifty-three years old at that time! I was certain that I would be the oldest person on the base—I was wrong. I served at the NATO Training Mission as the Deputy, Training and Operations for Intelligence to train, equip, and field Afghan National Army Intelligence Forces.

I worked with a great team of people from all branches of service and countries. I have stayed in touch with a few of my comrades. I especially enjoyed working with a Canadian colonel, who was an outstanding leader.

My mobilization left me with an intense appreciation for our country and our way of life. I hope the Afghans will be able to find peace to rebuild their country.

Following my mobilization, I was selected as the Executive Officer of the United States European Command 0167, Atlanta, GA, supporting Joint Analysis Center, Molesworth, England. This was a large unit of 125 people from all branches of service. It was a great opportunity to exercise leadership with a diverse group of patriots.

My final tour was Joint Intelligence Operations Center 0113, Minneapolis, MN, serving as the Training, Readiness, and Mobilization Department Head in support of Joint Intelligence Center, Honolulu, HI.

While in the Naval Reserves, I had many two-week tours in Japan, England, Germany, Guam, Okinawa, Puerto Rico, and Hawaii.

I was very happy to end my naval career with this awesome unit.

***

I retired with forty years and four days of service. It was time! I am very proud of my long service to our nation and to the United States

Navy. I received several personal and unit decorations during my career, including the Defense Meritorious Service Medal, the Meritorious Service Medal, Navy and Marine Corps Commendation Medals (3), Navy Good Conduct Award, and various unit and campaign awards.

I was also the recipient of the "OLD GI Bill" (Vietnam Era) that enabled me to earn an MBA and BS degree from Winona State University, Winona, MN, in 1989 and 1991, respectively.

***

Prior to 1976, women were not allowed to attend the military service academies. In 1976, this changed and it was huge! Why did it take so long? I often wonder what our nation lost in talent and service because of a law that did not allow women to attend and graduate from the service academies.

Wearing combat boots and being qualified on the M4 carbine infantry weapon and service rifle as well as the M9 semiautomatic Beretta 9mm pistol—there aren't too many grandmas who can claim these qualifications. In fact, the joke is, "Does your grandma wear combat boots?" My grandkids certainly can say, "Yes!"

I think there is a perception that women's military service is less than that of men; that our contributions are less than those of men. These perceptions are often built on the images and stories that the media shares via public forums. I believe these perceptions have led to a feeling of "invisibility" for many women veterans, which impacts them today, when in fact, they deserve the full honor and respect of this nation, and the public, for their service.

My message for American women is this: I gave four decades of my life to this wonderful country and I am very proud to have done so. Serving in our country's military is an honorable career choice! The opportunities are enormous. Whatever you can conceive, you can achieve. Anything is possible! Don't listen to naysayers. Don't listen to the negative comments about women serving in the military. Our Nation needs you! With the right attitude and focus, there is no limit to what you can do!

TWELVE

Kimberly Dobler

Kimberly Dobler
MN National Guard, 2000-2019

$\mathbf{M}$INNESOTA WAS MY first home. I was born on Jan. 28, 1983 to a single African American mother and a Caucasian father. I was five years old when my mother decided to move her children to Chicago, IL, to be closer to her immediate family.

I spent the majority of my adolescent years (5-13) in Chicago's educational system. There I witnessed drug abuse, gang violence, and interracial biased attitudes toward bi-racial children. Due to the violence of the community, my mother elected to return to Minnesota in 1997 so that her children could finish their education in a safer environment.

At the end of my junior year, a decision needed to be made on where to attend college and how to pay for it. Being in a low/middle class family, the ability to have my single parent pay for my education wasn't feasible. So, I researched scholarships and other opportunities. Ultimately, I applied and was accepted for some scholarships in my community. However, I needed guaranteed funds for my education.

I turned to the military. The males on my mother's side of the family joined, so I understood the obligation of service. I knew that I wanted to earn my education while at the same time serving my country. For me, the military was the logical choice. I joined the Minnesota National Guard during my senior year of high school.

I was the first female in my family on my mother's side to join the military. So I was fortunate that my family didn't chastise me for joining the reserves. They simply wanted me to do my best. The majority of my high school friends who joined the military did so for the same reason as I did.

I reported to Fort Jackson, SC, for Basic Training and AIT from July-Nov., 2001. I had enlisted into an administration specialist position. When I completed my ASVAB, my assigned recruiter asked me minutes before enlisting what type of job I wanted—"Signal" or "Human Resource." I chose Human Resource.

I was in a large room full of females who were primarily from the south. From my years growing up in Chicago, I was used to being called derogatory names for being bi-racial, and in that room I noticed the derogatory names increased. It wasn't until our black female drill sergeant overheard the issues that the matter was addressed and stopped.

On September 11, 2001, while I was at Basic Training, the Twin Towers in New York were hit. As a result, we were given the deployment briefing and status of movements weekly by the Garrison Commander and Command Sergeant Major. They were notifying us about deploying, so everyone was on alert regarding the potential of being deployed. After I completed my AIT, instead of deploying, I returned to Minnesota.

My mobilization was from June 2008–May 2009 to Al Asad Iraq, as sole Human Resource NCO for a MEDAVAC company supporting Marines.

As of August 2018, I have eighteen years of service. I have never regretted joining the military, but I will be pleased to reach twenty years. I am looking forward to completing this chapter of my life and starting one that will be 100% civilian.

Due to joining the military at a young age, there were many levels of discrimination that I had to overcome. There were times that I have felt dismissed. From age, beauty, and pre-conceived notions, there are times that I had to work harder so that I could be seen as competent, strong-willed, and not weak.

It was only recently that I labeled myself as a veteran. Previously, I never felt like a veteran because I believed that my responsibility in Iraq wasn't the same as the individuals within aviation. These individuals were risking their lives to retrieve injured Soldiers, Airmen, and Marines. In comparison, it was then that I felt "invisible." I eventually had to spend time with other female soldiers to understand my worth.

For American women, I would say this: Please do not judge the individuals who wear the uniform. If you are thinking of joining the military, do not let fear keep you from an opportunity.

Were there issues with the military? Yes, but I do not regret serving. I will have memories that will last a lifetime, and I would be honored if my daughter wanted to join.

WE ARE NOT INVISIBLE

THIRTEEN

Blair GreyBull

Blair GreyBull, Vietnam Woman Warrior
US Army, 1969

I WAS BORN ON the Standing Rock Indian Reservation in Cannon Ball, North Dakota. My life prior to military service was simply just trying to get by. I was aware that I was different because of my sexual orientation: a transgendered guy who liked to cross-dress! But one day I naturally made a "feminine" move and GrandDad saw me do that. He spoke to GrandMom in Lakota, telling her that it was not the thing to do! Although I was around six years old at the time, I knew exactly what was being said and realized that I had to change my ways. I had to be "invisible" way back then!

It was the early 1950s when, along with my brothers and sisters, I was shipped off to a boarding school in Pierre, South Dakota. It was very traumatic and lonely for us and we spent a lot of time crying for each other.

Often my one brother and I would climb to the top of the playground slide to see if we could catch a glimpse of our sister and brothers who were older and stayed in a different dormitory.

We got to go home in the summer, and that was the best time. Then in the fall, we all had to go back. I remember the buses that were there to transport us. There were lots of crying children and parents who were trying to comfort us.

Finally, we started to go to the "white schools." Then we had to deal with a whole set of new problems. Racism and poor quality education at the boarding school left us far behind in the classroom. In spite of the struggles, all of my siblings and I graduated from high school.

Following my graduation in the summer of 1968, the only option I saw for my future at that time was joining the military. The country was in turmoil, but I paid little attention then. I just wanted to seek adventure and travel the world.

Most of my family did not know I was thinking of signing up for military duty. My only problem was my speech impediment, so I wasn't sure I would be accepted. My older brother just happened to be home on leave from Vietnam. My mom asked him if he thought I could still enlist despite my speech problem. He said I could still sign up. So that fall, at eighteen, I volunteered for the draft.

In August of 1968 I was at the courthouse in Jamestown, North Dakota, with two other guys, and from there we were transported to Fargo. An Amtrak train took us to Seattle, Washington, and then on to Fort Lewis. We stayed in old-style military barracks. The first morning was a jolt to my senses when the drill instructor started to shout and bang on anything he could to wake us up! I could not believe where I was—"reality" was ice cold!

Since I had enlisted right after high school, I was in good physical shape, so Basic Training went by fast.

Then it was on to Advanced Infantry Training. While other guys were taking off to other countries, we were the "unfortunates," and we simply carried our gear across the street! I thought I would be going to some country other than Vietnam because my older brother was already there with the 82nd Airborne.

But much to my horror, I had orders to go to Vietnam. My knees buckled and I had to hold on to the chair! I felt that the war in Vietnam was wrong.

Early on a January morning of 1968, I arrived in Vietnam. It was chow time and I could only remember the smell of the red clay as I went through the food line. I had come in with two other new guys, and it didn't take long for us to be out in the "boonies" with our unit. Like my brother, I was assigned to the infantry.

***

After I was discharged from the Army in June of 1971, I went on a thirteen-year drunk! I felt guilty about my service because the Vietnamese were only protecting their way of life, much like my ancestors had done at Little Big Horn!

During this time, it seemed kind of surreal, trying to fit in with society. I bounced around from job to job, just waiting to get paid, then spending it all on drinks and drugs. I was wondering why so many veterans were having problems, but I found out later, when I finally sobered up!

Then all those PTSD symptoms came to the surface within me and I realized that I needed help— especially after my older brother committed suicide due to his time in Vietnam with the 82nd Airborne. During those short years of the early 1970s, we had never talked about our time in Vietnam. I would have loved to have been talking to him about our experiences.

I do feel better about my service now because of time and how it has changed my thinking. But I have attitude and anxiety problems today, and am still trying to connect with people.

I was so blessed with having met a woman in the early '80s. Then, after twenty-seven years of marriage, she passed away in 2012. So now it has been very lonely, trying to make friends, and especially to meet a wonderful woman once again!

But, as I said, I feel apart from people and it is very difficult to meet another special woman. It now looks like I will be spending another Xmas by myself.

The Great Spirit has been so merciful and forgiving, yet I am alone and really invisible. Some people fail to acknowledge my military service, and I feel like a ghost with my womanly features.

I sympathize with others who feel the same.

FOURTEEN

Sarah Guertin

Senior Airman Sarah Guertin
US Air Force, 1993-1996

*B*ORN IN THE small town of Granite Falls, Minnesota, on May 2, 1974, I was the youngest of three children. I was only one when my paternal grandparents were killed in a car accident and my parents took in my eight-year-old uncle to raise as their own. My father was an elementary school teacher who loved camping and hiking. We spent most of our early years outside learning. My mother stayed home with us kids. I couldn't have asked for a better childhood.

Then my teen years changed my perspective on our world. I was sexually attacked by a "friend." I became a very angry young woman and began to drink heavily. This would be a struggle for many years after.

When I was in my first year of college, at Worthington Community College (now Minnesota West) I was falling behind in my grades and sinking further into a deep hole due to the trauma from my teen years. An upper-class friend of mine, who I admired dearly, was leaving for basic military training and we talked about my possibilities and what I could do to help my situation. I recalled talking to military recruiters while in high school, and I always found the Air Force to be the branch that would best fit my needs. So, when my friend convinced me to change my life around, there was no question about my path forward. At that moment I decided to join the Air Force. At age nineteen I went to the recruiter's office the next day and signed up. I left a month later.

My dad was a little upset with me for dropping out of college, but the day I left for basic training he was more than supportive of my decision. Anyone who knew me well enough knew that this was something I would be good at. I've always been a very strong, independent person and it was only fitting that I do something out of the norm for a woman.

I was headed for Lackland Air Force Base in Texas by June 4, 1993 for basic training. This training was a whirlwind of emotions and developing strength, both mental and physical. I was in a flight of fifty and graduated with twenty-six. Our drill instructor was a very strong daughter of a Marine and we called her "Iron Fist." She was the first strong military female in my life. We graduated as an honor flight, beating out our brother flight for the honor. This was a great feat for us young women.

On the 4th of July, we were allowed to leave our quarters after dark, and from under the overhang, we enjoyed fireworks. It was in this moment that I realized the honor and importance of what I was taking part in.

From Texas, I was sent to my permanent base at Vandenberg AFB in Santa Barbara County, CA. A few short months later, I was sent to Georgia for training. Every place I had been so far had been in large groups, but this time I was alone. Now, for a young, inexperienced nineteen-year-old, this was scary. As my small puddle jumper was taxiing down the runway, the nice gentleman seated next to me asked where I was headed. While I explained where and why I was headed, I kept thinking this gentleman looked very familiar. As I tried to place his face, I was explaining to him how the Air Force works and what my job was. Then it came to me—this man is General Lord, the Commander of Vandenberg! I had just been explaining how the Air Force works to a general! I then asked him if he was who I thought he was. He was. As the plane landed, he said, "God speed" and that he would be keeping an eye on me.

Fast forward a few months when I was back at Vandenberg. I was invited by a friend to attend the Officers' Christmas Ball as his date. As a result, I was allowed to wear civilian clothes, not dress blues. My friend was a very high-strung individual who was a little nervous about how I might behave in front of his superiors. I reassured him that I knew how to behave in front of officers. When we walked into the ballroom, there was a welcome line of all the top officers in command. As we worked our way down the line, there stood General Lord. He reached for my hand and said, "Hello Airman Guertin." My friend's jaw fell toward the floor and he no longer questioned my ability to impress. (As for myself—I was impressed that the general remembered me!)

My career field was chosen for me before I went in the service. I was chosen to be a Reservationist at Billeting (lodging for soldiers in civilian homes or other non-military facility.) It was a great honor to be selected for this position and it gave me wonderful opportunities to be involved with many committees around the base.

I was involved in the 1995 Space & Missile Competition-Guardian Challenge. I helped with the housing of hundreds of officers who were traveling to compete in the Challenge. I was also the main contact for housing the Thunder Birds when they came to our base for an airshow. I got to pick up the pilots and their crew from the flight line and bring them to their housing units. This position gave me VIP access to the airshow. It was a very fun event to be involved in.

In support of Operation Sea Signal Joint Task Force 160, I was deployed to Guantanamo Bay, Cuba in 1996. It was beautiful. But upon arrival to our camp, all of the Army guys came out of their hooches as we walked down "Fresh Meat Alley." This was something that female vets had to endure, whether you wanted to or not.

As an adult female victim of past trauma, I now look at that experience differently. At the time, I was in a male-dominated world and just brushed this off as "boys will be boys." Now I look at it with disgust. My fellow female soldiers and I had to be briefed on how to conduct ourselves while there. We were informed that the ratio was one female to every twenty males. We were not to walk or go anywhere alone. When I reflect back on this, it seems sad that you have to warn female soldiers that they are the weak link in the military chain—not because they can't do the same job as their male counterparts, but because they are "Female."

Cuba is a beautiful country, and an experience not many U.S. civilians can say they've had. Overall, my time in Cuba was very positive. I enjoyed getting to watch other branches of the service work together, and I made some great memories with my fellow soldiers.

I spent approximately three months in support of the Marine and Army troops there policing the Cuban refugees. As a flight, our purpose at the camp was to run the dining hall, maintain the gym equipment, and run billeting for all personnel in the camp. I worked overnights in the billeting trailer.

Toward the end of our deployment, we helped tear down the camp.

***

Due to overmanned numbers at the time, I got out of my contract eleven months early. When asked to re-enlist, I chose not to. I was ready to go home and I took advantage of the opportunity. I was discharged on July 8, 1996.

I sometimes wish my older self could have told my younger self to stick with it, but things are what they are. I struggled for a few years after my return to civilian life. The adjustment was not an easy one, but I found my way and stayed on my path of becoming the person I was meant to be - not the person my attacker created those years back. And I can thank the USAF for the strength and knowledge.

When I look back on my time in the service, I feel pride, honor, and joy. My experience in the service was a true positive for me. It gave me the skills and knowledge I needed to grow up and become the person I am today.

I currently work with veterans on a daily basis as an Assistant VSO (Veterans Services Officer) for Chippewa County, and I get asked daily if I am a veteran. This can be frustrating at times, but I have learned to go along with it. Getting recognized as a woman veteran is something I've always fought to have and with the IANI campaign, I feel full of pride to be a part of it. We are not "invisible."

My message to other American women veterans is this: Hold your head up high as a woman and know you have more strength inside you than you could ever imagine. And don't let anyone take that away from you.

WE ARE NOT INVISIBLE

FIFTEEN

Catherine Hutchison

1st Lieutenant Catherine Hutchison
US Army, 2011-2014

I was born the third of three girls and our home was in Edina, Minnesota. My family life was rather structured and discipline was strict. As an individual I thrived on knowing and meeting expectations and adhering to routine. I was very obedient and rarely got in trouble. I had respect for the rules in place and respected authority. I grew up in a Christian home where service to others and to the community were values instilled in us from an early age. I went on mission trips to housing projects in Chicago, Aruba, and twice to Juarez, Mexico.

I was also physically active from a young age. I tried nearly every sport I could play. Basketball became my primary sport throughout most of my adolescence and later I turned to track and cross-country.

My family is full of over-achievers. My grandfather, after serving in WWII, worked as the Assistant Director of the FBI and the head of the FBI's Identification Unit. My mother's mother was unable to attend college, so she pursued stenography and became a secretary. While living in Washington, D.C., she served as the secretary to Senator Danforth. My mother graduated undergrad with a BS in Physical Therapy and worked as a PT for two years before pursuing medical school. She graduated at the top of her class at Wake Forest. She became a Physical Medicine and Rehabilitation Specialist and worked as the Medical Director of Cancer Rehab and Lymphedema at Allina Health, serving on two national boards. My father worked in health care consulting for more than twenty years and went to graduate school to get his MBA. He left consulting to start his own financial planning business. Essentially self-taught, he studied and passed the certification exams. Eighteen years later, he sold his business for a large profit and continues to independently consult. These examples of achievement gave me a strong belief in hard work, facing challenges, and pursuing your goals with intensity and determination.

As I got older, I developed an obsessive interest in military institutes such as the Air Force Academy and Virginia Military Institute. My attention focused on applying and getting admitted to college for nursing, and Bethel had accepted me for a Bachelor's in that field. Still, I was lured to the military, and so I visited the Marine recruiting office. I learned that the Marines do not have nurses. A friend informed me about the Reserve Officer Training Corps, where you could join the military and simultaneously attend college for nursing. I soon met with the UofM Army ROTC recruiter. The opportunities specifically for nurses simply could not be matched in the civilian world. I was impressed with the physically grueling aspect of the program as well.

My father's father served in WWII in the Army Air Force as a rear gunner in B-29s, my mother's father served in the 106th infantry division in the Ardennes after D-Day, and my mother's uncle served in WWII and received a battlefield commission in North Africa. Despite this rich history of service during WWII, there was no direct military influence or presence in my life, other than hearing an occasional story. No other family members served between their generation and me.

Both of my parents were surprised and proud of my decision and always supported whatever goals I set for myself, but my mother seemed apprehensive. Once it became clear that this was something I wanted to do, they were 100% on board.

I joined ROTC at age eighteen after high school graduation and began the program concurrently as I started my four years of nursing school. ROTC training included physical fitness training three mornings a week at 6:00 a.m., and cadets were enrolled in military science classes, where we were taught the Army values, leadership skills, staff organization, battle drills, land navigation, and military history. In addition, one weekend a month we attended training exercises that included practice battle drills, operations orders, and leadership of a squad in battlefield scenarios. Then we had to qualify at the range, perform day and night land navigation, or test our combat water survival skills. I also participated in the drill team, practicing close-order drill and ceremony with arms. ROTC was my priority and many other typical campus-based activities fell by the wayside.

During the third year of ROTC, nursing cadets are sent to a United States Army Medical Center to participate in the Army's nursing program, called Nurse Summer Training Program (NSTP), which I attended at Ft. Bragg, NC. I had been interested in Obstetrics since high school and was able to do my internship on the postpartum unit at Womack Army Medical Center, taking care of women and infants after delivery. This program under the supervision of an RN, allows nursing cadets valuable experience that civilian nurses typically don't experience until their first job. Following the thirty-day internship, I flew to Ft. Lewis, WA, for the Leadership Development and Assessment Course (LDAC), another thirty-day course. This one involved testing and evaluation of learned skills and leadership abilities for cadets from around the nation.

The score received at LDAC holds great weight in determining a cadet's branch of service and location of first duty. I studied intently during those months, and my preparation paid off. I received perfect scores in land navigation and on the Army PT test. After scoring 320 out of 300 on the APFT (Army Physical Fitness Test), the commander refused to believe that I had run two miles in under fourteen minutes. Overall, I was given an "E" which stands for "exceeds expectations," and I graduated fourth out of 800 cadets in my rotation.

Following my four years of Army ROTC training, I received my officer commission and joined the Army as a second lieutenant (2LT) and was sent to the Army Medical Department (AMEDD) Basic Officer Leader Course (BOLC) at Ft. Sam Houston, San Antonio, TX. I was placed in this training as a Registered Nurse after graduating with my BSN from Bethel University. The first week, classes covered Army programs such as Sexual Assault and Harassment, Equal Opportunity, common acronyms, and Army doctrine. Following the classroom portion, officers had field training exercises such as requesting and providing MedEvac, as well as setting up and operating a Battalion Aid Station and Combat Support Hospital. We also had to pass the Army Physical Fitness Test (AFPT). We were informed that officers with the top five PT scores would be allowed to attend Combatives Level 1 Training to learn the basics of hand-to-hand combat and receive a certification if you passed. I scored 300 out of 300 possible points. The top five scores in my platoon were all achieved by female officers, and I had the fourth highest PT score. Once our platoon leader learned that the top five scores were all female, he announced that he was selecting the top three females and the top two males to make it "fair," and I was no longer awarded the opportunity to attend combatives.

This made me very angry. If five females out-performed all of the males in the platoon, those females should be rewarded for their effort and achievement. I am certain that if the top scorers were all male, this same adjustment would not have taken place. My achievement went unrecognized and unrewarded in the manner originally promised.

We had the weekends off and often officers would explore San Antonio, the River Walk, local bars or restaurants, or have barbecues behind our lodging.

One month and three days into training there, I attended a barbecue behind our hotel with members of my platoon as well as other members of the company. That evening, I was raped by two (identified) and one (unidentified) male officers from another platoon.

I told my roommate what had happened to me and she told me that I needed to report the incident to my platoon leader. I did, and his first response was, "Why were you separated from your battle buddy?" Further into our discussion, he stated that he would talk to my rapists' platoon leader to "sort things out," but assumed it would be a "he said, she said" situation. I waited to see what would happen.

The following week, we returned to the field, where I had to see my rapists on a daily basis. I began experiencing panic attacks, extreme anxiety, and poor mental functioning. I again told my roommate about my troubles. She immediately walked me over to our platoon's victim advocate, who asked why, if I had reported it, nothing had been done. We were perplexed.

She asked if I had undergone a medical examination, which I hadn't.

Because it was still within seventy-two hours, she rushed me to a local hospital. I underwent a SANE (Sexual Assault Nurse Examiner) exam where clear evidence of trauma was observed and documented. She then helped file my unrestricted report of the incident.

This opened an investigation by the CID (Criminal Investigation Division) and I was subject to hours of questioning, had to provide my clothing, bedding, and other belongings for evidence in the case. The investigator's plan to get the male officers to admit to the rape was to try to re-entice them through text messaging. This made me very uncomfortable but I complied. It did not work. They next attempted the same thing by having me make a monitored phone call. Due to the panic attacks, I refused and began to realize this was revictimizing me. They eventually interrogated the two identified rapists, who both admitted to the act, but claimed that it was consensual. Considering that I was intermittently unconscious from the suspected drugged drink they provided me, it was not possible for me to consent. DNA from my underwear confirmed DNA from both of them.

The investigation continued throughout the remaining weeks of my training. The CID process itself was contributing to the frequency of my panic attacks, and the CID officer told me it was unlikely there would be a conviction after all. It was at that point that I withdrew my participation in the investigation so that I could move on and focus my attention to training and my first job as a nurse. This incident overshadowed the entire remainder of my training. My platoon leader did not follow protocol and he ignored the report of my rape. The two identified (married) men both had admitted to the sexual assault, yet nothing happened to either officer and they were able to continue on with their military careers without even a black mark.

By the time I finished BOLC (Basic Officer Leaders Course), three months into my service, I was angry, resentful, anxious, depressed, and having difficulty coping. Upon graduation from BOLC, I was sent to my first duty station at Ft. Bragg, NC. After arriving in early November, 2011, I rented an apartment alone, off base and commuted five minutes to the hospital on base. Prior to receiving a permanent job assignment in the hospital, new graduate nurses participated in three clinical rotations (two to four weeks each), on the medical-surgical floor, the surgical floor, and postpartum.

Following these rotations, we requested our preferred unit. I requested postpartum since I had always wanted to work in labor and delivery, and I knew that starting on postpartum would give me preliminary OB experience to reach that goal. Womack Medical Center at Ft. Bragg is one of the larger MEDCENs for deliveries, averaging about 300 babies born per month. I would gain invaluable experience at this location, preparing me for my career in OB nursing.

Nearly immediately after arriving at Ft. Bragg, my inability to cope with the aftermath of my rape became apparent. I developed several autoimmune diseases, likely set off by the stress of the event. I developed Hashimoto's thyroiditis and losing weight became difficult. To add to the problem, I also developed binge eating disorder to numb the feelings which added to the weight problem. My sleep became erratic and I woke every two to three hours.

I sought counseling at Ft. Bragg to address the depression, panic attacks, and sleep issues. Just as my rape had been ignored by my platoon leader, the medical psychiatrist told me, "This might be your new normal," and taught me deep breathing and visualization, but never addressed the underlying trauma (despite me telling her I had been raped). Every mental health professional I saw while on active duty didn't address the rape.

My weight became an even larger barrier to my service at that time. The Army had "height and weight tables" used to gauge body fat for soldiers who may be deemed overweight. Through their use of a tape measure and a rudimentary formula, I fluctuated only 1-3% over their standard at that time and was therefore held back from my promotion. Despite having a 300/300 on my PT tests, I was required to go to remedial physical training to manage my weight. But exercise and physical capability clearly was not the problem. Yet no one was addressing the real problem. So I was punished for my weight despite my superior performance. This made me even more stressed and hopeless.

I obsessively focused on my weight under the constant threat of "getting kicked out" due to being overweight. This intensified my eating disorder. Despite good APFT scores and optimal performance reviews in nursing, I was unable to get my "automatic" promotion to first lieutenant (1LT) due to my weight. I was also unable to attend the specialty course for labor and delivery due to my weight. No one was helping me to overcome the incident that had severely scarred me. I felt further betrayed by the Army in that I was being held back because of my weight despite good performance in all other areas.

After one year at Ft. Bragg, I was offered a rare opportunity to work in Labor and Delivery at the General Leonard Wood Army Community Hospital in Ft. Leonard Wood, MO.

Due to my weight, ordinarily I would not have been able to attend the required sixteen-week OBGYN course in order to work as a labor and delivery nurse. But, because Ft. Leonard Wood had a very small community hospital and was in need of nurses, they made an exception because I had postpartum training and was willing to come to that duty station. I was thrilled to finally be learning the specialty I always wanted to work in. It took a while, but I eventually felt truly comfortable with my coworkers. They became like family, and I loved where I worked.

However, my weight continued to be a problem, and many of my PTSD symptoms continued untreated. I had difficulty managing all the competing priorities of nursing, the Army, remedial activities, and personal life. I was still unable to receive my promotion and continued to be forced to attend remedial PT. "Making weight" consumed me and accelerated all of my physical and mental health issues.

By the time I was discharged from the Army in September of 2014, I had a minimum of two medical appointments each week and was on fourteen different medications. I was medically discharged through a process known as Med Board, which determines service-connected disabilities and discharges you with medical compensation. It was clear that PTSD was still a problem in multiple areas of my life and I had developed physical injuries from extreme exercise. For these reasons, the Med Board ensured that I had all the medical benefits I needed to care for myself in the civilian world, and I felt relieved.

I was ready to move on to the next chapter. But I also immediately felt lost. The military lifestyle had been my life, and fellow cadets and officers had been my family for the last seven years.

Despite some of the military's failings, it is organized and structured so it feels familiar wherever you go. Even though you may not know everyone, the military can feel small and you feel like you are part of an exclusive patriotic club. You speak the same language, wear the same uniform, practice the same customs, and greet one another.

But, once you're out, you're *out*. This made me feel a distinct loneliness I was not prepared for. I also had no idea where my life was headed now that the military was no longer part of the picture. I went from feeling scared to excited, resentful, relieved, angry, happy, and everything in between. I think I was also grieving a military experience that was nothing like the one I had hoped for back in that ROTC recruiting office at eighteen years old. It was difficult to come to terms with the reality of my time in service.

***

I am still healing from my time in service. However, the time I have spent healing myself has helped me to be proud. I served my country. I was an officer in the United States Army. I helped bring hundreds of babies into the world, including some over Facetime with deployed parents. I was compassionate, hardworking, determined, and resilient.

However, I still feel a knot in the pit of my stomach about feeling "invisible." I felt invisible because my rape was ignored, downplayed, and not prosecuted. I felt invisible because none of my other accomplishments mattered because of the number on the scale. I felt invisible in ROTC because my accomplishments there were ignored and never verbally acknowledged.

My feats were verbally doubted by my commander or met with snide remarks that diminished my achievements.

When I was discharged from the Army, I felt invisible to the civilian world. In the Army, enlisted soldiers salute officers, and junior officers salute senior officers. I was saluted and called "ma'am." My rank was acknowledged. You could tell from the uniform who someone was in a military sense. I had a clear place in the system. However, once I was out, I was just another person on the street. My existence had no outward display of my achievements or who I was and what I do in this world. No one knew I was a veteran or a nurse. I felt invisible and alone in the world.

I also felt invisible when discussing my service or that I was a veteran. At a local store when asking for a military discount, they would thank my dad for his service (he has never served.)

When I tell people that I served in the Army, they act surprised and sometimes ask again just to make sure I meant what I said. All of this contributes to the feeling of invisibility.

***

Following my discharge from the Army, I was offered a GS nursing position in labor and delivery. Basically, they offered me my job as a civilian. Then a remarkable offer came from Missouri Baptist Hospital, working with high-risk patients, allowing me an opportunity to practice in a more acute setting.

While I loved the job and the friends I made, the city wasn't the right fit for me so after six months, I moved back to Minnesota where I was offered a job at the Mother Baby Center at Abbott Northwestern Hospital. It was always my dream to work there after the military. I worked Labor and Delivery there from 2015-2017, and in the summer of 2018, I began working exclusively with our high-risk antepartum patients

I am pleased to say that I have now reclaimed my visibility as a service member. I no longer rely on others to validate my service. I have decided to be proud of my service. I have turned my anger and resentment into an opportunity to share my story. Every year on September 25, I share on social media a letter I wrote about my rape to publicly tell my story and to let other women know that they are not alone. Through sharing my story, I hope to promote change. I feel like this was the purpose of my service. While it may not have been everything I hoped it to be at the time, I think I am making a much bigger impact in using the story of my rape than if I would have had a mundane course in the military.

I have also stayed connected to important friends from my time in ROTC and the Army.

I discovered the "I Am Not Invisible" campaign and knew I had to share my story. This was yet another opportunity to connect with veterans, specifically female veterans who have or sill are feeling "invisible" about their military service, and it was a beautiful experience. I am thankful for the fellow veterans I met in the process.

My messages for other American women are these:

To women who have served: Your service matters. No matter how much you were or weren't recognized or rewarded for your accomplishments, they still happened. You did that. You are a rare breed of woman even when the world refuses to appreciate you."

To the women who have been sexually assaulted or abused:

Reclaim your life. It was not theirs to take. Don't let them keep you stuck. You are not alone. Find help, find healing, and find your inner strength. No one can take what has been with you all along. As Judge Rosemarie Aquilina said to the many sexually-assaulted gymnasts, "Leave your pain here and go out and do your magnificent things."

For women with an eating disorder: The single most important day of your life is the day you decide once and for all that you are enough and that you deserve to take up space in the world.

For women everywhere: What is the greatest lesson a woman should learn? That since day one, she's already had everything she needs within herself. It's the world that convinced her she did not.

WE ARE NOT INVISIBLE

SIXTEEN

Diane (Meyer) Keith

Sergeant Diane (Meyer) Keith
US Air Force, 1969-1973

*B*EING THE SECOND oldest of nine children came with much re-sponsibility. I was raised on a large farm near Cooperstown, North Dakota. My parents worked very hard, and we all had jobs to do to help them. Most of our food came from our farm. My mother canned much our food from our huge garden.

I went to a country school until sixth grade when the little school closed and we had to go to school in town, which was a huge change. Our farm was a mile off the main road and winters were so brutal! On stormy days, my dad would take us to meet the school bus (which was an old 1949 station wagon). Dad would harness two old work horses to a wooden sleigh, and my sisters, brothers and I would pile in, pulling a quilt over our heads to keep from freezing. Life on the prairie was very tough to navigate in the winter, but we survived.

We moved from North Dakota to South Dakota during my junior year in high school, and that was a tough transition. I had been thinking about going into the military for a couple of years, and the move from North Dakota kind of solidified my decision as our new place in South Dakota just did not feel like home to me.

I wanted to be sure this was my best choice, so I decided to take a year after graduation to just have fun and experience life without a lot of restrictions and no schedules. I went to Seattle with a former classmate and worked enough to have some spending money.

Her parents lived in a suburb of Seattle called Kent, Washington. I was able to stay with them so that I was able to save a lot of money.

As time moved on, I realized I had to "get a real job," and at nineteen, I went to see an Air Force recruiter. I had heard that the Air Force was the best branch of the military for women. Before you knew it, I had enlisted. It would end up being a great, life-changing decision.

My older sister got married right out of high school and had children right away. I saw the challenges she faced as a young wife and mother and decided that was not for me. My siblings were sad of course, that I was going away, but they were all busy with school and their activities, so to them it was also something exciting to tell their friends. My parents were ok with my decision, while my friends had mixed reactions—some happy, some not.

I flew to San Antonio, TX, in January 1969 for Basic Training. I went to a designated area at the airport to meet up with others who were headed to training by taking the bus from the airport to Lackland AFB. After those of us who were headed for Lackland had boarded the bus, a drill sergeant jumped on as we were leaving and he started barking orders right away, such as "DO NOT TALK TO OTHERS!" and "SIT and LOOK STRAIGHT AHEAD!" I was shocked and scared and wondered if I had made the right choice. I think this was just due to fear of the unknown.

I really wanted to go home at that point. I don't remember how long the ride was, but I do remember getting to the dorm on the base, and then the fun began. We were given specific instructions as to what was going to happen the next day. I think I just dropped into bed and fell asleep to escape, because I knew that for the next six weeks, I would be exhausted!

The exhaustion started early (6:00 a.m.) the following morning, as we had to "fall in" outside the dorm and march across the base to get shots and our uniforms. We stood in line and they came out with an "air gun" which they used to give shots. Some people flinched, and if you did, you got a huge tear in your arm. My arm got real stiff and ached right away. Then we had to march back to the dormitory, carrying a heavy duffel bag. I remember thinking how much I wanted to go home. Some of the girls cried a lot.

It was a very warm January and we had to go to the drill pad for marching. We marched a lot every day. We had to learn the correct way to make a corner (square, not round), and we had to learn to all be in sync during the marching. It was grueling. Some of the gals would actually pass out because it was so hot. I was so short that I was always in the front of the squad and I was easy to spot if I was out of step.

When it was my turn to stand CQ (Charge of Quarters) for two hours during the middle of the night, I remember being so darned sleep-deprived, then having to go back to sleep for only a couple of hours.

Then I had to get up and be out on the sidewalk at 5:00 a.m. and march across the base to chow. We had to get our food, look straight ahead, and not talk to each other during mealtime.

We had to take turns cleaning the latrines with toothbrushes around the toilets and we also had to buff the floors. One time I was buffing the CO's (Commanding Officer) office and the buffer machine got away from me. She was at her desk when the buffer hit it. The desk moved, and she was sitting there as her desk moved away. I got yelled at, then she said, "Airman Meyer, you are done buffing!" She got someone else to finish the job.

I was sent to the chow hall to peel huge piles of potatoes and also do KP (Kitchen Patrol), which involves emptying the slop off the plates. It was disgusting!

We would have mail call once a week for the first three weeks and getting a letter from home was the best, but it also made me more homesick. At the end of the third week, we could make a five-minute collect call home from the pay phone down at the end of the dorm hall. I cried the whole five minutes that I was on the phone.

As time went on and we developed friendships with the other WAFs (Women Air Force), life got easier. We even had facial makeup classes as part of our training. I already wore makeup, so for me it was fun, but for some of the young women it was an education, as they had never worn makeup.

Some of the women flunked out because they could not handle the rigorous training and the discipline. I kept telling myself that each day done was another day behind me as I worked my way through Basic.

One night while in bed, I was writing a letter under my blanket when it was past "lights out" time. The drill instructor made an unannounced visit and caught me. She said, "Airman Meyer! In my office at 0800 hours!" When I got to her office the following morning, she asked why I was not following orders. I told her I was homesick and that was why I was writing. For not obeying the rules, I lost phone privilege for that week.

At the time I was in the service, most people smoked, so we would have to go on "butt patrol" and pick up the dang cigarette butts people threw on the ground. We had to have our toothpaste and the limited toiletries we had lined up in our cupboard according to size. During inspection, if they were not properly aligned, we were written up.

Too many write-ups and you could be set back in training. Our beds had to be made in the military style. The drill instructor would bounce a quarter on the bed and if it was not made tight enough, the quarter did not bounce and you got written up. We had to spit-shine our shoes with cotton balls and starch our shirts so they would stand on the floor. All the Basic uniforms we wore were cotton and if there were any wrinkles in our chambray shirts, that was a write-up.

The highlight was graduation from Basic Training, and I cannot describe the pride I felt that day.

We marched in front of a group of high-ranking officers, and we did it with perfection. All that grueling time on the drill pad paid off at last!

After Basic Training, my first duty station was at Travis AFB, California. It was a great location, sixty miles east of San Francisco. I started to enjoy my service and had a nice time during my two years there. I worked at the Military Airlift Command in the training department, which provided pilot training in simulator and in flight. There were times when I and another female Airman were allowed to go "out in the field" to the actual training. We never "wet-ditched" out of the planes, but were able to go with them when they were training to jump out of the planes. My duties were administrative in nature but I got involved in all aspects of pilot training as well.

I was part of a "Welcome Home" committee at Travis AFB when some of the first POWs came home from Vietnam, which is a highlight of my Air Force enlistment. I can still see the faces of the family members of the POWs as they saw them for the first time, getting off the plane and walking across the tarmac! I even had the opportunity to fly to Hickam AFB, Hawaii, for a few days, accompanying the crew that was heading there for training. Before being transferred to Chicksands RAF England, I received the Air Force Commendation Medal, which is an honor I am most proud of.

In 1971, I was stationed overseas at a security base which was forty miles north of London. I had a top-secret security clearance as I was working with highly-classified information in the intelligence area while stationed overseas at the 6950th Security Group. I also worked for the base commander in an administrative support role and I became friends with his family and babysat their children.

I met a lot of wonderful people, both British and American, with whom I stayed in touch for years. I traveled around Europe a lot on the weekends and during time off. Some of the countries I traveled to included Scotland, Austria, Germany, Belgium, Wales, and Ireland. On the way over to the UK I met and befriended another Air Force WAF and we are still friends today. We got together in Washington, D.C., about five years ago after not seeing each other for thirty-five years. We went to the Women's Military Museum and enjoyed a wonderful reunion.

***

During the period of time that I served in the military, women were often treated disrespectfully. There was a lot of sexual harassment that we were subjected to. There was harassment by high-ranking enlisted men and officers as well. At that time, there was no support network for women to turn to. Much of the time, the harassers were people that we reported to, so they used the power of their position to keep us quiet. While I did not experience it personally, some women experienced military sexual trauma (MST) and have suffered from the effects of it.

I was discharged from the Air Force in January 1973. At that time, I was more than ready to come back to the US. I was homesick and had enough of the military. Of course, in time those feelings changed.

I bought a red MG sports car while in England and had it shipped home to California. I moved to Minneapolis a year later, met my husband, and married. I had a son, and when he was two, I enlisted in the Army Reserve at Fort Snelling. I was also in the reserves for two years, then was discharged.

When I ended my enlistment, I really didn't talk about it that much since at that time, people were not interested in hearing about it. My years of service were dismissed and faded to "invisible." It was not at all a country of patriotism, but a greatly divided country when it came to war.

My former husband was in Vietnam and has suffered the physical and emotional scars of war, which have had a negative impact on his life.

Now that our country is more patriotic and is trying to make up for the awful treatment of men and women who were in Vietnam, it is such a joy and honor to be a veteran. Finally, some of the respect due to those veterans is being shown, but for women veterans, we still have a way to go.

My message for other women is this: If you are a veteran, please stand tall and proud. You deserve the recognition and respect that as sisters in arms we sometimes do not feel.

Speak out about the harassment you have been through and do not allow yourself to be victimized by this.

Stay involved with other women veterans and participate in events that allow you to share your experience with them.

Men are gradually accepting that women are now equal in the service, so in that regard it is getting easier. The same can be said in the civilian world, and that is women are at last, in most cases, receiving pay equal to that of men for the same jobs. This has only happened in the past few years, and in some cases, still not!

Stand up for each other as women and build each other up. We are not invisible!

WE ARE NOT INVISIBLE

SEVENTEEN

Cindy Larson

Chief Petty Officer Cindy Larson
US Navy, 1974-1994

I WAS BORN in Sacramento, California in 1954. My mother (Gala) married my father, Raynard, who was in the Navy. When his tour was complete, I was four years old and we moved to his home state of Minnesota. We had a house north of the Twin Cities.

In 1972, I was about to graduate from North Branch High School, but I was not yet ready to go to college as I didn't know what I wanted to do. I worked a variety of jobs, but felt like I wanted to see more of the country outside of Minnesota.

I had seen commercials on TV about the different branches of the service and I decided to join the Navy since that was the branch that my father had served in. Also, by serving I would be qualified for the GI Bill to go to college. I planned on doing my four-year enlistment and then getting out.

My family and friends weren't thrilled with the idea of my decision to serve in the military since there were very few, if any women who we knew that had been in the service. However, when I entered, they were very supportive of me.

I was inducted into the Navy in January 1974 at the age of nineteen. I was sent to Basic Training in Orlando, FL. I was thrilled as I left Minnesota during the winter and I was headed for summer-like weather in Florida.

I arrived at Basic Training wearing heels and a dress. I tripped while going down the bus stairs, and I landed on my hands and knees!

I looked up, and my soon-to-be CO (Company Commander) looked at me and said, "Oh God! Not another one!" I think I then realized that this was going to be a whole different experience for me.

Basic Training was mostly classes and physical training. At that time, women did not learn to shoot weapons or anything like that. From Basic Training I went to Great Lakes, Illinois for Hospital Corpsman training since I had chosen the medical field as something I had an interest in. From there I was stationed in Jacksonville, FL.

As I was nearing the end of my tour and time in the Navy, a chief petty officer talked to me about going to Advanced Training and extending my time in the Navy. He was persuasive and convinced me to go to Basic Lab Technician School, which was in Portsmouth, VA.

After I finished that school, I had orders to Guantanamo Bay, Cuba, but I was granted a thirty-day leave and I went home. After four weeks, I took a MAC (Military Airlift Command) flight to Cuba. I was very surprised when I arrived. I was asked what I was doing there since my orders had been changed while I was on leave. I spent a week there before I flew back to Portsmouth, VA, for duty.

As I was nearing the end of my tour there, I decided to go to Advanced Medical Laboratory Technician School which was in Bethesda, MD. When I finished there, I was sent to Rhode Island to work in the lab at the hospital, then stationed in San Diego, CA, where I attended Drug and Alcohol Counselor School.

I also completed my Bachelor's Degree in Psychology during this time, using my military benefits.

I have the distinction of serving twenty years in the Navy and never being stationed overseas, although I requested it repeatedly. I did get to serve on a ship though. I was part of the pre-commissioning crew for the USNS *Comfort* T-AH-20. This was an extremely rewarding assignment. I had the responsibility of setting up the laboratory aboard this 1,000-bed floating hospital. After we were commissioned, I was part of the crew that took that ship through the Panama Canal to our homeport in Baltimore, MD. I feel such a sense of pride when I have seen it mobilized for different disasters over the years.

***

I retired from the Navy in 1994 after serving twenty years. I was tired of moving every few years and ready to do something different in my life. At the time I retired, I simply looked at it as a job I had done for two decades. You didn't hear much about veterans at that time. I basically walked away from the military feeling like I had done a good job.

For many years, I was "invisible" as a veteran. Few people knew I had served in the military. I didn't have contact with veterans' organizations and really didn't associate with other veterans. I didn't call myself a veteran until I started to work for the Minnesota Assistance Council for Veterans, an organization that serves veterans. Also, Afghanistan and Iraq were battlegrounds our troops were involved in, and there was much more recognition of veterans.

Through work, I became involved in two women veterans' groups in Minnesota and I started meeting with other women veterans. I still do feel "invisible" sometimes as when at veterans' events I often get asked if my husband has served.

My message to other American women is this: Military service is a wonderful way to serve our country. There are so many opportunities in the service for women now. It helped me to grow into the woman I am, and most days I really like who I've become—and the Navy was a big part of that.

EIGHTEEN

Laura J. Ludwig

Colonel Laura J. Ludwig
US Army, Army Reserve,
Army National Guard, 1975-2011

*A*S THE OLDEST of seven girls, I had many responsibilities around the house. My mother stayed home with us, while my dad was the Vice-President of NBC, channel 11. We lived in a northern suburb of Minneapolis, and I would have to always be watching my younger siblings.

I had jobs since I was thirteen, working on a farm, babysitting, then at McDonalds. I was a tomboy and enjoyed participating in many sports.

I lead a sheltered life, but by the time I reached my teens, I was anxious to be an adult and out of the house, ready to explore the world. I wanted to leave home, but the question was—how could I support myself? In my senior year at Osseo High School, I knew I wanted to go to college someday, but again, how would I pay for it?

The Vietnam war was just wrapping up and recruiters were still trying to meet their quotas. The military would house me, feed me, clothe me, pay me, and teach me a marketable skill to use in civilian life. Also, the college benefits and VA loan eligibility were very enticing. My father was a high-ranking officer in the National Guard and I always admired him in his formal dress uniform, looking so handsome and strong. I have fond memories of ironing my dad's fatigues sprayed with liquid starch and pressing the corners razor sharp. Little did I know that one day I would be pressing my own uniform!

In 1975, you could sign up for the Minnesota National Guard at 17.5 years old and go to Basic Training after graduation. In the interim, you could go to drill and get paid! The path forward was obvious. Following in my dad's footsteps, I chose the Army, (even though the Navy had cuter uniforms.)

My high school friends were shocked. Why would I want to join something so unpopular as the military? I was laughed at and my boyfriend was angry. My mom cried, but I was confident in my decision. With just a two-year commitment, I would have money in the bank, a marketable skill, and other military benefits.

About five months before my high school graduation, I was 17.5 years old and I enlisted in the National Guard. I was sworn in at the Minneapolis Armory on 15 January, 1975. My dad read the oath and swore me into service to my country. I remember my dad's face—a combination of pride mixed with paternal fear/protectiveness. He knew the unpredictable consequences and dangers of serving in uniform.

I left for Basic Training at Fort Jackson, SC, in the summer of 1975 after turning eighteen.

I smugly thought I was an adult, so worldly and experienced. Was I ever naive! Growing up in the '70s and going to school in Osseo, Minnesota, was a "Wonder Bread" existence—a White, Caucasian, Swedish Meatballs, Lefse, Heterosexual, Middle-Class lifestyle. No diversity in my world! This did not prepare me well for the reality check that was to come at the Reception Station in Fort Jackson.

My dad took me to the airport that morning, his innocent little girl, going off to Basic Training, and it was time to have "the talk." He sat me down and tried in his gruff manner to enlighten me on what to expect. I didn't make sense of his talking about not getting too close to anybody, to watch my back—especially in open showers. WHAT??? I assured him that I was training with other girls. He answered, "That is what I am talking about." I was clueless.

The Reception Station at Fort Jackson was a culture shock. What a melting pot of colors, socio-economic backgrounds, orientations, religions, and accents—all wearing the same uniform. My best friend and Battle Buddy was a sassy black woman from the ghettos of New York with an accent I could barely understand. Try explaining to her what a Minnesota hot-dish and Jello salad were all about!

I was assigned to Battalion Echo 18-5. The time and training during Boot Camp bonded each individual into a team member. It was difficult, but I learned to bite my tongue and not to roll my eyes in formation. Drill sergeants do not appreciate "eye rolling!"

Once, back when I had been fifteen, I was learning to drive and I got angry at my dad when he insisted that I learn how to drive a manual transmission. Forward to the first week of Basic Training, and the troops were asked who could drive a stick-shift jeep. When I was the only one who raised a hand, I became the Battalion Driver. The reward was, if you were the Battalion Driver, you were exempt from KP (Kitchen Patrol—keep peeling).

My Advanced Individual Training was at Fort Sam Houston, San Antonio, TX. I was trained in the medical field as a 91 Bravo (Combat Medic) with additional training as a 91 Delta (Surgical Technician), learning to deal with carnage, mutilated and mangled bodies, and dying young people. Most critical and difficult was having to make life and death triage decisions.

I loved my black leather combat boots. I spent hours with polish, spit-shining them to an almost patent-leather sheen. While my fatigues were soaking in liquid starch, I worked on the toes and heels of my black jump boots—spitting and buffing, spitting and buffing, until they gleamed. You were considered a "strack" soldier (one who keeps perfect uniforms, above standards) based on your boots. It was a source of honor and pride to be complimented on your boots during inspection.

Then the Army issued tan suede combat boots to go with the DCUs (Desert Combat Uniforms.) Suede? Low maintenance—"Just use a brush to clean away the dirt and sand," we were told. Well, brushing might help with the sand, but it did not help in the medical environment where I worked. At the FOBs (Forward Operating Bases), being part of a FST (Forward Surgical Team), we worked in Triage and the Operating Room (OR). At times, our uniforms and boots were soaked with blood and other bodily fluids from the injured. I tried wearing OR shoe covers, but they would work their way off. I also tried wearing garbage bags over my boots, and taped them below my knees, but it was dangerous as I slip-slided around, moving from patient to patient. I had to give up on trying to clean my suede boots. You can never scrub or spit shine the tan suede boots or clean off the spilled blood of our warrior heroes. Those blood stains are a permanent reminder of the ultimate sacrifice, and the horrors of war.

I was a young, eighteen-year-old private, just finishing up my MOS training as a surgical technician. I enjoyed being in the military, and I had just been honored by receiving a congressional nomination to West Point Military Academy. My dad was so proud!

However, that dream ended the day I elected to stay late after my shift at the hospital in order to finish taking care of the patient I was assigned to.

Usually, the squad returned to the barracks as a group, but because I stayed late, it was just turning dark when I started the walk alone. Suddenly, from out of nowhere, I was roughly thrown to the ground. It knocked the breath out of me, as I tried to process what was going on. Thrashing around with his weight holding me down and a hand clamped over my mouth, I could not believe what was happening to me. At 4'11" and about 116 pounds, I was no match for my assailant. My screams were muffled in the back of my throat. He never spoke. Struggle or fight? Struggle or fight? Or submit?

I remember then hearing the distinctive snap of a switchblade being flicked open and the feel of the cold steel blade against my inner thigh. I remember the pungent, sickening smell of body odor mixed with cologne. Then, suddenly, he jumped up and ran off! I lay there stunned, looking up at the sky and trying to piece together what had just happened. Did he hear something? Change his mind? Reconsidered the consequences? I pulled myself up and headed back to the hospital to report the assault.

I had just experienced an attempted sexual assault and my sense of personal security was shattered. I felt violated, but that was nothing compared to the dismissive attitude and shaming I endured when trying to file a report. Instead of being treated like a victim, I was figuratively "raped" and stripped of any personal dignity by the very system I thought would protect me. The assault had only lasted about two minutes, and I have a small, one-inch scar on my left inner thigh as a distant reminder of how lucky I was.

However, the betrayal of the military authorities caused long-lasting psychological damage and altered the course of my Army career, as I decided against West Point. How could I break barriers in a traditional all-male academy when I would be terrified of my classmates and instructors?

After serving two years of active duty as an Operating Room Specialist, I returned to Minnesota as a reserve component soldier. I worked as a Surgical Technician while attending nursing school, then getting my associate degree at a community college.

I completed my undergraduate work for a BSN with the University of Minnesota.

In 1977, I was selected for Officer Candidate School (OCS), Minnesota Military Academy, one of the first class of cadets open for women. I graduated from OCS with honors and was awarded the Top Academic Award and runner-up Leadership Award. I was commissioned as a second lieutenant in the Women's Army Corp as a WAC, Medical Service Corp Officer. Additionally, I was recruited to be the first female training officer on staff at Minnesota OCS Academy, serving for three years, teaching military history, military leadership, tactics, marksmanship, and physical training. At the OCS Academy, I mentored, counseled and advised cadets, grooming them toward commissioning to become future leaders of military service. After my assignment at the academy, I served in several command and leadership positions in the Medical Battalion with the Minnesota National Guard. In 1992, I transferred from the Minnesota National Guard to the Army Reserve component, as an Army Nurse Corp officer.

As a drilling reservist, I continued my civilian education by being accepted in 1983 for a Masters graduate program in Nurse Anesthesia at the Minneapolis School of Anesthesia. Upon graduation in 1985, I accepted a Staff CRNA (Certified Registered Nurse Anesthetist) position at Methodist Hospital, Minneapolis, MN.

My military education includes OCS, Basic and Advanced Medical Service Corps Officer Courses, Medical Management of NBC Casualty Course, the C4 Combat Casualty Care Course, CAS-3-Combined Advanced Staff Service School, and the Command and General Staff War College.

Over the years, I was mobilized to active duty for multiple deployments:

2003 – Mobilized and deployed in support of Operation Iraqi Freedom. Assigned to the 801s Combat Support Hospital in Kuwait and served as the Chief CRNA.

2006 – Mobilized and deployed again in support of OIF and Operation Enduring Freedom. Assigned as staff CRNA to Landstuhl Regional Medical Center LRMC. Was requested to extend mobilization and served 36 months at LRMC, providing anesthesia to the wounded warriors.

2009 – Deployed nine months to Afghanistan in support of Operation Enduring Freedom, assigned to the 30th MEDCOM. Sole anesthesia provider at two FOBs and three months at Craig Joint Forces Hospital in Bagram.

2010 – Requested by name to return to LRMC as Chief CRNA and European Consultant for an eighteen-month assignment.

During multiple deployments over the years, I personally faced challenges of my own from loneliness, isolation, fear, and separation from my family.

Toward the end of my service, at fifty-five years of age, trying to keep up with the young soldiers and living in harsh conditions became increasingly difficult. Imagine three tall, strong, strapping young men and 4'11" me, carrying a 200-pound patient on a litter and running to the waiting helicopter.

I missed the comforts of home—like privacy, electricity, running water, and personal safety. I was one of a few women attached to this unit, and I believe I was the oldest person on the FOB at that time. As a high-ranking officer, I felt like a social pariah. I recall one day while sitting in the dining tent eating my lunch, several young soldiers came in and set down their trays on the table. One of them glanced at me, noticed my rank, then they all picked up their trays and moved to a different table. Ouch! Nobody wants to socialize or be friends with the boss—the one who writes your evaluations, conducts inspections, reads your charts, and recommends you for promotion—or not. The only time I felt welcome was in the middle of trauma situations, where we functioned as a team and my skills were vital. I dealt with compassion fatigue and multiple challenges to my moral compass. These are some of the "Invisible Wounds of War."

People often ask me how it was to be deployed downrange in a combat zone. I can talk and show photos, but that is so one dimensional. To fully understand, you have to be immersed in the environment with all of your senses: the comingled smells of blood, gun powder, dirt, body odors, infected flesh, and death. To hear the rotors of the helicopter overhead, and the distant sound of incoming mortar fire mixing with the keening screams of the wounded. To view mutilated or missing extremities, the sight of the trauma inflicted from an IED that exploded upward between the legs of a soldier, to look in the terrified eyes of a nineteen-year-old casualty and watch it be replaced with a blank stare as his soul leaves his bloodied body. You are aware of your own visceral responses, the beads of perspiration trickling down your back, tasting the bile coming up your throat, and you can feel your own heart beat racing with fear for your own safety. But, you have to block this sensory overload and *focus.*

You fall back on your trauma training and you do your job. Over and over, caring for the injured, until exhausted, you fall into your cot. Sleep comes to you, but the traumatic smells, sights and sounds invade your dreams and play a macabre looped movie in your head. This nightmare recurs days, months and years to follow.

***

In July, 2011, I retired after 36.5 years of military service. I continued to serve through an assignment to Iraq with the United States Department of State as an anesthesia consultant.

Somehow, a two-year commitment had stretched into a thirty-six-year career.

I am proud to have worn the uniform. I am proud of my identity. There were obstacles, and there were sacrifices. But I knew in my heart that I had made a difference with competent and compassionate care of our wounded. I may have retired, but I am a Soldier for Life.

***

When I returned home alone, there were no Welcome Home ceremonies or parades. It was surreal leaving a chaotic and frightening environment, then stepping into the ho-hum civilian world. It was similar to when a teenager leaves a violent video game and then goes to the refrigerator. When I was in the military, I was a respected, powerful, high-ranking officer with in-demand critical skills. The military had structure and a clear chain of command.

Now that I am retired and not wearing the uniform, I am not part of that elite club anymore. I don't get to sit at the "cool kids" table. My identity had been wrapped around my military role, and now I need to reinvent myself because I have felt my service is invisible. I didn't realize that reintegration would be so difficult.

[Colonel Ludwig's awards include the EFMB (Expert Field Medical Badge), The Legion of Merit, Afghanistan Campaign Medal with Star, Meritorious Service Medal (2nd award), Army Commendation Medal, (3rd award), Army Achievement Medal (5th award), Meritorious Unit Commendation Ribbon, US Navy Achievement Medal, Army Reserve Components Achievement Service Medal (3rd award), Good Conduct

Medal, Global War on Terrorism Expeditionary Medal, Global War on Terrorism Service Medal, Army Service Ribbon, Overseas Training Ribbon, Armed Forces Reserve Medal with M device (3rd award), and the NATO Medal. She currently works as a staff CRNA at Methodist Hospital in St. Louis Park, MN. Although retired from the military, she continues to be deeply interested in veteran issues. She serves as Vice Chair of the Women Veterans Initiative. At the VA Hospital in Minneapolis, COL Ludwig has a chair on their advisory board. She is a member of the American Legion, VFW, Veteran Golf Association, the Patriot Guard, the Combat Veterans Motorcycle Association, and the Eagles Group (a network of veterans and veteran-friendly corporate executives that help transitioning military personnel with job-seeking skills). COL Ludwig is very involved with the Eagles Healing Nest organization in Sauk Center, for housing and healing homeless veterans and she currently volunteers with Haven4Heroes in Anoka, MN, renovating buildings for homeless veterans.

She is the mother of two daughters, Molly and Chelsey, and a grandmother of three.]

Her message to others is this: Reported cases of military sexual assault are just the tip of a very large iceberg. Unless all women and vulnerable others come forward and report incidents without fear of shame or retaliation, the problem will continue to exist."

Also, this quote by an anonymous WWII Army Nurse: "Let the generations know that women in uniform also guaranteed their freedom. That our resolve was just as great as the brave men who stood among us. And with victory.. our hearts were just as full and beat just as fast—that the tears fell just as hard—for those we left behind."

As a final aside from Colonel Laura Ludwig, she proclaimed: "I am proud to say that in my thirty-six years of service, I never had KP or peeled a potato!"

WE ARE NOT INVISIBLE

NINETEEN

Betty Jeanne Mahaffey

Commander Betty Jeanne Mahaffey
US Navy, 1969-1992

*A*T A NAVAL hospital in Pensacola, FL, I was born the oldest of six children. My dad was a blimp pilot who served twenty years in the Navy. We moved a lot when I was young, but then remained stable in New Jersey near Lakehurst Naval Air Station where the blimps were based. We stayed there from the time I was in third grade until I graduated from high school. There were four children in our family until I was eleven and mother had another. Two years later, she had one more, and I helped care for them.

I went to one year of liberal arts college in Missouri after high school graduation, but I was homesick for my family. I returned to New Jersey to attend nursing school. I was inspired by TV movies of the wars and the military nurses and the Bob Hope specials from overseas. After seeing the hospital ship, the *Hope* on TV endorsements, I wanted to be a nurse and work on a hospital ship, traveling to see the world while caring for people. I then knew I wanted to follow in my dad's footsteps and join the Navy where I could do both travel and nursing. My family was supportive since they knew I wanted to travel.

While doing my pediatric rotation in Philadelphia, I went to the Navy recruiting station and signed up. My father swore me into the Navy. He was so proud to do that.

I was twenty-two years old when I was inducted into the Navy, then sent to Newport, RI, for my Officer Candidate School training. I was there from October–December 1969. We learned Navy history, leadership, military law, plus many other military basics. From there, I was sent to Great Lakes Naval Hospital, where I worked in labor and delivery.

One year later, I received orders to the USS *Sanctuary*, the hospital ship off the coast of Vietnam. I always said that was when I went from "Babies to the Battlefield!"

Soon after arriving on the *Sanctuary*, we learned that the ship would be returning home as the war was winding down. We left Danang on 1 May 1971 and brought the ship back to San Francisco. I took some family leave, then went to the island of Guam for two years. While there, I worked in labor and delivery at night, and evenings were spent working on the MED EVAC wards when the nightly buses came in with our injured Vietnam vets on their way home to the States for further treatment and recovery.

At the end of my two years, I went to Portsmouth Naval Hospital in Virginia for the OB/GYN Nurse Practitioner Course, and worked in the emergency room and OB/GYN clinics prior to the start of school.

At the end of that school, I was sent to Rota, Spain, for three years, where I provided OB/GYN care to active duty and dependents, delivered many babies, and taught Lamaze classes.

From Spain, my next duty station was Pensacola, FL, where I worked in OB/GYN clinics and labor and delivery. I was responsible for training the Family Practice Residents Normal OB care and Normal Labor and

Delivery. I was there for three years before I was sent to Newport, RI, where I again provided OB/GYN care, including delivering babies, to our active duty and dependent women.

My final duty station was a return to Pensacola, where I continued to provide OB/GYN care to active duty and dependent women. I have also served as the Specialty Advisor to the Navy Surgeon General for Nurse Midwives and OB/GYN Nurse Practitioners.

Each new duty afforded me many new experiences and long-lasting friends that I will always remember. The opportunity to see the Pacific and Europe as well as the USA are things I will never forget.

I retired from the Navy in Pensacola in 1992 after twenty-two years of service.

***

Following my military retirement, I soon entered another form of service. My mother was diagnosed with dementia. My father's wish was to keep her at home, so I helped him care for my mom for ten years until his death. Then I continued with my mother's care for six more years until she passed away. I was so thankful to be able to be there for my parents, just as they had been there for me and my five siblings.

Since my mother's death in 2013, I became active in the Midwest Navy Nurse Corps group in Minnesota. I also volunteer with two church groups, making quilts for missions and for our veterans. I also sew baby bibs, blankets, and burb cloths for new moms in our Women Veterans Clinic. I am an active member of the Joint Retiree Activity Board, that plans the annual Retiree Activity Day which brings our retirees up to date on their benefits.

My latest highlight was the opportunity to go on the Twin Cities Honor Flight to take seventy-eight WWII and Korean era veterans to Washington, D.C., to see their memorials. It was a very touching and emotional experience.

***

I have so many fond memories of my Navy career. There are many lasting friendships. Yet there have been some "invisible moments," for example, when someone sees my Vietnam Vet license plate and says, "Thank your husband for his service."

TWENTY

Richelle (Couillard) Nelson

Sergeant Richelle (Couillard) Nelson
US Army Reserve, 2002-2010

*I*T WAS THE day before Halloween in 1983 when I became the third child to my parents; they had adopted my older twin sisters from India. About a year and a half after my birth, our family welcomed another girl. We grew up as a family of six in White Bear Lake, Minnesota.

My sisters and I were not only close in age, but we were also close friends. We bonded over our love of soccer, *The Price Is Right* show, and summers when we had not a worry in sight. To this day we all still play soccer together. We are a very family-oriented group. We did everything together: meals, activities, church, soccer, trips, celebrations, etc. As cliché as it sounds, we were the average middle-class American family. I feel very blessed and fortunate to have grown up in the family that I did.

I knew I wanted to go to college after high school, but I also knew the military was an option. My sisters and I were raised to have respect for our Armed Forces: it just came natural to us knowing that our dad and other family members had served. Multiple generations in my family served in the military, mostly Marines. I was always inspired by their courage and bravery to serve in past wars, including WWII, Korea and Vietnam. I wanted to become a Marine but I didn't think I had it in me to make it through their Boot Camp.

I learned that I could join the Army as a Reservist and then go to college. I also liked being physically active and I knew that Basic Training would push me to become even more physically fit. I was determined that I could do it and I was very excited to make it happen. I was also proud of myself for doing something different right after high school. The military option was not a foreign concept in our family, therefore, everyone was very supportive. My friends took it harder than my family did. I am sure my mom was nervous about my decision, but along with everyone else, she was part of my great support system.

Right after graduating from high school at age eighteen, a good friend and I joined the Army Reserves in June 2002. We reported to Fort Jackson, SC for Basic Combat Training (BCT) that following fall, in November 2002. It was really nice to go to BCT with my friend. I'll admit I cried the first night of BCT. I immediately second-guessed my decision to join; however, I became accustomed to the new way of life very quickly. I learned that if you mind your own business and don't volunteer too much – things would be okay. Oh – and don't eat the desserts or drink the pop you see in the dining facilities (D-FAC). Some failed to follow those instructions, and then we would all be punished in the "front leaning rest position" (aka pushups) downward on a hill immediately after the meal outside the D-FAC.

I will never forget the final Field Exercise and Ruck March at the end of BCT. It was beyond grueling- it was the hardest physical obstacle in my life at the time. Who knew it would end up snowing in South Carolina in January? Not me! I'm sure my experience was nothing compared to those who served in the Korean War, and you would think a girl from Minnesota would be well-prepared for some snow, but I wasn't.

We dug fox holes and had "shelter halves" for tents in the field. A Shelter Half is where you and your Battle Buddy each have half a tent; you button them together and you have a tent barely big enough for two. These tents were nothing but a slab of canvas. All I had to do was survive a few nights in the cold & snow, eat some MRE's, carry out tactical maneuvers, and guard the perimeter, all of which I managed. Then it was time for the march back. It was horrendous. It was a good 10-15 miles out and the same going back. My body was physically and mentally drained. I was aching so badly, I had visions of graduating in a wheelchair, literally going across the stage in a wheelchair! As we neared the end point on the march, a burst of energy and fulfillment entered my soul and I felt a great sense of pride and joy that I was almost done with the final task of BCT! And then we made it back to the barracks, the finish line. I could not believe it. I felt so powerful in that moment, and I think of that moment often; it brings chills from my head to my toes.

When I look back at my BCT, I believe it was truly an amazing experience. I gained new life skills, improved my Physical Training (PT), touched and used weapons for the first time in my life, threw a grenade, climbed over obstacles —literally and metaphorically, formed life-long friendships with Battle Buddies, and most importantly, became a committed soldier in the US Army.

The cold and snow cleared up and Graduation Day was warm and sunny in South Carolina at the end of January 2003. My parents and younger sister were able to attend the ceremony. Upon completion of Family Day and BCT Graduation, I was shipped north on a bus to Fort Lee, VA, along with many others who were heading for logistical job training, Advanced Individual Training (AIT).

Upon enlisting back in 2002, I was given a handful of MOS (Military Occupational Specialty) options. Looking back, I should have rallied for something more along the lines of a career I was actually interested in. I knew, however, that my chosen MOS was just temporary—eight years temporary that is. However, when it comes to wartime, I knew I would do whatever job is needed, so any job really worked for me. I chose to train as an Automated Logistical Specialist, (92A).

AIT was a lot more laid-back than BCT. After just a couple weeks of AIT, we earned civilian passes on the weekends where we could go off post for the entire weekend. One thing was certain—fun was had by all! My Battle Buddy and I even got matching butterfly tattoos one weekend. I enjoyed the routine at AIT; it was similar to going to high school or college. We did PT in the morning, went to class, lunch, then more classes. Evenings were usually for studying, cleaning the barracks, and hanging out. My instructors were mostly civilians and that made it feel more like college. There was one instructor in particular that really stood out; he was a very good instructor; he also meant business. One day I got in trouble for putting my legs up on a chair as if it were an ottoman. I was days away from completing AIT and I thought I got to the point where that would be okay. Well, I quickly learned that I was still a soldier in training and that was NOT appropriate! My punishment was to write a "Chair Essay," explaining why I should not raise my legs onto the chair. The instructor threatened that I would not graduate if I didn't write this essay. I got to work on it right away! I told my parents about this incident—they got a chuckle out of it! My dad still has possession of the "Chair Essay," that I wrote and the incident has become a running joke in my family ever since.

Soon it was time to graduate from AIT in April of 2003. I was very sad because I loved my platoon, my company, and the friendships I formed but it was time to officially become a 92A; an official soldier of the US Army. Graduation was at the end of April in 2003 in Fort Lee, VA. My mom was able to attend graduation. She got to meet my friends and she even got to meet the girl with the matching butterfly tattoo. I then headed home and officially became a member of the US Army Reserve with the 19th CMMC in Arden Hills, MN.

The 19th CMMC's first modern-day deployment was in 2003, when the USA invaded Iraq. I was in BCT at the time so I missed that deployment. Fast forward to 2005 and the 19th CMMC was called up again for the same war, same mission. I deployed in October 2005 with the 19th CMMC out of Arden Hills, MN to LSA Anaconda in Balad, Iraq. We were primarily a logistics/supply unit. This was the second time the unit was deployed for the Iraqi War on Terrorism. Those who had deployed in 2003 had the choice to deploy again or not. Those of us that did not deploy in the first go around were automatically on the list to deploy this time around. Most of the soldiers who deployed in "Round 1" decided not to deploy again since it was such a quick turnaround, which meant we had to fill a lot of holes in the Unit.

The Army has what we call "cross-levels," where the Army randomly selects individuals from all over the US to join our unit. Most of the cross-levels came from the Midwest, others from farther distances. This was actually a blessing in disguise, meeting all those new faces, some of whom have become my best friends to this day.

Once our cross-levels made it to Minnesota, we began training and then shipped off to Fort McCoy for a six-week training in August of 2005. During that time, some of us were sent to out-of-state bases for MOS refresher courses. I was one of them. I went to Georgia, and it was kind of fun to get away during this time. Upon coming back to Fort McCoy, we were granted a weekend pass. My family picked me up and we headed for the Wisconsin Dells. It was really nice to have some family time before the year-long deployment.

In early October of 2005, the 19th CMMC packed up our lives into duffle bags and foot lockers, loaded up and headed on a commercial jet occupied by military only to Kuwait. Once there, we spent about a week doing some final training before heading "north." Upon completion of training in Kuwait, my boots landed via a C-130 in Balad, Iraq, on approximately 4 October 2005 in the middle of the night.

I will never forget the helicopter landing and then stepping off of the plane. I could not believe it—I WAS IN A WAR ZONE! I remember I was *very* afraid to get off that C-130 but I knew I was meant to be there; I knew no matter what happened to me that is what I was called to do. I took a deep breath, had trust in my fellow comrades, got off the aircraft, and set out for the year-long mission. We were herded to the transition barracks, and by barracks I mean slabs of wood nailed together to make somewhat of a structure. We were briefed on how the transition would go and what the next steps would be.

We eventually moved into our hooches as we called them. Our hooches were basically a trailer home structure divided into three sections. Each section was shared by two soldiers. My hooch was not exactly close to work or the dining facility. Our base was quite large. I took a small bus to & from work. Our shower facilities were in a different trailer home-type structure. Most days we had warm water, some days we did not. Our base had many amenities; laundry service, a movie theater, an outdoor pool, a running track, fast food restaurants, coffee shops, a shopping bazaar, barber, gyms and recreational centers. I was able to play in an indoor soccer league and swam outside as much as possible in my free time.

I worked the night shift, so I slept during the day. We started off by working every single day, twelve hours a day. My job was exactly what I trained for in AIT. I processed and approved supply requests for units in Iraq. I mostly dealt with building material supplies such as wood and tools, as well as cold weather supplies. It was a fairly easy, not-too-stressful job. The only stress was when mortars would fly in, mostly during the night while I was working. Our base was nicknamed "Mortaritaville." The name fit very well, unfortunately. We also did tower guard duty. There were about thirty towers surrounding our base, and our unit was responsible to man about three of them, twenty-four hours a day.

After a couple of months, when we had our jobs and tasks under control, we started to get one day off work per week. It was nice to finally not work seven days a week. I liked my work schedule because while I was working during the night in Iraq, my family was up in America as it was their day-time. I was able to call home frequently via calling cards. I vividly remember getting to do a video conference with my family one night while I was deployed. It was so wonderful to see their faces and for them to see mine!

After spending seven months in Iraq, just past the half-way point of my deployment, I was granted a two-week leave; I could travel anywhere in the world. I chose to go home. I surprised my mom for Mother's Day and I surprised my sister on her actual twenty-first birthday! This was one of the best days of my life. My mom freaked out when she saw me, and my sister was cautiously shocked and quite confused. My leave was amazing. I crammed a lot in and during my two weeks at home in Minnesota; I saw a lot of friends and family. Two weeks came to an end quickly and I was on my way back to Iraq. It was hard going back to war after such a good time at home, but I knew I only had about four or five months before we would be relieved by the incoming unit.

Eventually, our twelve-month deployment was nearing an end. The unit that relieved us showed up and settled in. We trained them for about a week, then we were relieved of our mission. It was time to head back to the USA!

On 19 September 2006, the 19th CMMC landed at Fort McCoy, Wisconsin, where many families and friends were waiting. It was a very powerful feeling—landing on US soil after my first (and only) deployment. I was so relieved that I came back alive and well, as did my fellow soldier friends. The deployment was overall a good experience. I can't believe I served in a war and made it home. I am very fortunate and proud.

In July 2008, I was eligible to join the Inactive Ready Reserve (IRR). While in the IRR I did not have to attend the monthly Battle Assembly nor participate in the Annual (two-week) Training. I joined the IRR while I was pursuing my college degree. I left the Army Reserves when my eight-year contract was complete in July of 2010.

At this time, I had become a Radiologic Technologist and had been working as one for two years when my contract ended in July of 2010. Not even a year after I was out of the Army/IRR, I met a guy on www.okcupid.com, who eventually became my husband! We married in 2013 and now hope to become parents through adoption.

I was very proud of my service. I made a lot of lifelong friends and became skilled in ways I never thought I would be, but at the same time I felt ready to move on—ready to take on the veteran status and get on with my civilian life. To this day I wonder what it would have been like if I had decided to stay in. I do miss the military being a part of my life, but at the end of the day I think I made the right choice for myself and my future.

***

It's hard for me to believe I served in the United States Army Reserve.

The majority of people I know (other than my family) have no military background, which makes me feel like an outcast at times. My family, close friends, and coworkers are well aware of my service and make a point to recognize my service when the topic arises. When the topic does arise though, I get a little anxious and frozen, as if my service doesn't count because I am a female, or because I didn't do convoys on deployment, or that I did my service for eight years then stopped. Those thoughts race through my head. In those times I try to remind myself that my service does count. I did serve.

Although I am proud of my service, it's hard for me to stand up and speak about it and at times it seems as if it didn't happen. Strangers definitely have a hard time believing that I served. While I was serving I think I was more apt to speak out about it and display my story, but now that I'm out I feel like I must keep it to myself and remain "invisible" about my service, even though in reality I know that's not the case.

My message for other American women is this: We are equal! Made differently, but we are equal. We can do anything we set out to do, whether it's in the military or in the civilian world. Don't be shy, do what you want to do. Make a difference in the world—it can be big or small, but go out and do something. Be strong, stand your ground, be proud and be determined!

TWENTY-ONE

Amber Nielsen

Specialist Amber Nielsen
WI Army National Guard, 2002-2005

*T*EXAS WAS NOT my home for long. I was born in Austin on December 11, 1984 to Linda Frost and Robert Wateland. After I was bitten by fire ants, then had to stay in the hospital swollen from head to toe, we moved closer to family in Montevideo, MN. My brother Shawn was born there in 1989.

We moved to St. Cloud, MN, for a short time before my parents separated; then, my mother, brother, and I moved to Webb Lake, WI. My younger childhood was not a "normal" one, with many struggles which created some of the trust issues I still deal with today. However, they are part of who I am and what has made me stronger.

I was a straight-A student until my sophomore year in high school when I decided to start hanging out with the wrong group of people. My best friend, Holly, told me how stupid I was being, but also said that when I was done with the others, she would be there for me. I started smoking, drinking, going to parties, and spending time with people that didn't have my best interest at heart. I kept my grades up for the most part because I knew that was going to be my ticket out of a small town; however, it wasn't easy battling with the person I knew I should be and the person I was becoming.

In the summer of 2001, I decided it was time to get my act together. It wasn't until those two towers fell on September 11 that my world stopped. Watching that happen showed me that the world is so much larger than myself and the small town I was accustomed to. Everyone was silent.

I was in the library of my high school, getting ready for the school day to start. The rest of the day consisted of traveling from classroom to classroom, watching the television in each one as history unfolded before our eyes. I remember going to the office to call my mom, who started crying as she turned on the TV at home.

It wasn't three weeks past the towers falling when recruiters came to our school from every branch of the military to pitch the military to seventeen- and eighteen-year-olds and stress why it was important for them to serve their country. Holly and I sat next to each other, listening as he explained that the Army National Guard would not only train you and let you continue to live daily until called upon, but they would also pay for your college tuition. My friend and I came from families that could not afford to pay for college.

My grandfather had served in WWII. Nobody else on my mother's side had signed up. On my father's side, I have uncles who both proudly served our country.

My friend and I wanted to defend our country, our friends, family, and strangers we didn't even know. We also wanted to set up our futures. The National Guard won us over and we went home to tell our parents. They were nervous to sign us over at the age of seventeen, but proud and willing to do so. Also, I had two brothers, one older and one younger—both proud yet fearful. Soldiers were being deployed every month and the possibility of that was high.

Holly and I enlisted, then drilled with our National Guard unit throughout most of our senior year.

Two weeks after our high school graduation in June 2003, Holly and I left for Basic Training. It was nerve-wracking, to say the least, because it was becoming "real." As we had completed our senior year, we had also been drilling with the 724 Engineer Battalion. This unit deployed while we were in our senior year, however, due to the fact that we hadn't completed Basic, AIT, or high school, we were not deployed with them.

Instead, we were sent to Fort Jackson, SC. It was hot and the dreadful fire ants were everywhere, plus the drill sergeant did nothing but yell! It certainly was a shock to the system, but it didn't take long to get used to it.

On our third or fourth drill, we went into the woods and were doing ambush-type training with paint guns. Holly and I found a great place to hide behind a fallen log. While we got bored waiting for someone to find us, we took off our Kevlar and noticed a bunch of slits in it. We brainstormed what they could be for. Then we decided to put sticks and twigs in them to make ourselves less visible and more like a tree. Our commander was the first person to find us, and I recall to this day his deep tone in which you could not tell if he was angry or not: "Privates! What are you doing?" We really did not know how to answer, but finally I replied, "Trying to figure out what these slits are for, and we thought this helped us hide better." After making us wait for what seemed like eternity, he smiled and said, "That is exactly what those slits are for!"

Basic Training, to me, was actually fun, for the most part. Holly and I ended up being squad leaders. Working out, team building, sleeplessness, obstacle courses, firing weapons, etc. all became part of a "normal" routine. Being apart from my family was probably the hardest part, as I had never been away for that long or that far.

Getting yelled at by men was also something that took me some time to get used to. I wasn't accustomed to it at all, and quite frankly, it scared me. I didn't like the feeling of someone having control over me, but I grew to understand it was all a part of the "break you down and build you back up" system. Having my best friend since sixth grade at my side made things a million times easier.

AIT was a whole different field! We were both designated 63Bravo: Light Weight Diesel Mechanics. This was determined by our ASVAB test scores and chosen prior to swearing in.

At AIT, we had a bit more freedom, a smaller room with about six girls, and female drill sergeants who actually yelled more than the men. It always felt like they believed they had to prove themselves to get respect in a "man's world." After a month or so, we were able to get passes to leave on the weekend, which we spent relaxing.

After Basic Training and AIT, we naturally felt a bit more a part of the group as we had "graduated" and gone through all the trials and tribulations it takes to be broken down and built back up as a soldier.

We were able to help others who were coming in. It is like walking through the doors of a high school for the first time—you don't know where you are going to fit in, if you will be accepted, and as a woman, what you will have to prove.

The 724 was not this type of unit. I very much looked forward to our drill weekends. It was a time that we all got to get together—like a family reunion every month.

Two- week trainings during the summer consisted of shooting on the range (least favorite) and re-qualifications. Vehicles were moved and worked on and there were various classes.

Prior to our unit coming home, we also had the experience of going to Louisiana for our two-week training to assist in training a unit from Texas that was heading overseas. Holly and I had to dress like Iraqi women; only our eyes were visible for most of the day. It put into perspective how different another culture could be. We were in a building separate from other units for about a week at a "camp" that was a mock city much like there would have been in Iraq. That was my favorite two-week training during my service.

***

A year after starting college, I met my husband, Eiler. He had two children who I have always thought of as my own. Their biological mother was an addict and was very emotionally abusive toward them. The word "step" doesn't exist in my mind, just as the word "half" doesn't exist with my brother Jacob or my sister Rebecca.

After I became pregnant with our son, Camden, Eiler and I decided that I should honorably discharge. It wasn't just because of the pregnancy, but also because the kids' counselor had said that I was the kids' emotional stability and removing me from them for a period of time while deployed would be detrimental to their health and well-being as I was a "positive and nurturing role model of what a mother should be."

I also had a sergeant who encouraged me to choose this path because he had seen how hard it was for his kids to watch his wife deploy.

Still, it was not an easy decision. It was not the path I had planned when I joined. I enlisted to protect and serve my country, before all else. However, after meeting my children and becoming their mother, my heart couldn't leave them as I felt they needed me more. Being pregnant and gaining two children changed my perspective since I then was responsible for tiny lives who had my whole heart.

Staying on call in the IRR was not all that bad, until I had ten days of IRR service remaining when I received orders to go to Iraq!

I hadn't trained for nearly two years or been active, and they were deploying me for eighteen months in a unit I was unfamiliar with. Of course, fear set in.

My husband and I were both in school, we had two children at home who needed me, he was working mornings at UPS as a pre-loader, and I was serving at Applebee's.

My being removed from the house would vastly change the dynamics of everything. My husband would either have had to drop out of school with only one year left until he had his degree or quit the job he had that provided our family with full medical coverage. It was very stressful, to say the least.

We filed a petition. All of my family, including my grandfather who understands commitment to our country when you take an oath, wrote letters supporting the fact that I was needed more at home than I was overseas at this point, especially with only ten days remaining in my contract.

Three days after getting the paperwork back that I was not being sent as agreed upon by the military board, I found out that I was eight weeks pregnant with our daughter.

Still, it was not easy signing the discharge papers. I wasn't just leaving a job; I was leaving a family. Our unit was filled with amazing men and women.

After going on Inactive Ready Reserve, it took a long time for my months to feel normal. Not having to go to drill, and seeing the parking lot full during the weekends they were drilling, was difficult because I had gotten out before Holly. Knowing that she was still in was the hardest part of all because I felt like I had deserted her.

Holly and I had been part of a unit that worked together as brothers and sisters. We were all there for the same reason. I questioned my decision to leave for months/years after. To this day, I still feel as though I gave up on a promise I had made to my country. However, I have come to accept the fact that I made the right decision.

***

I have been a fifth-grade teacher for nine years. It is my passion and I believe that I make a difference every day that I am in the classroom.

The military acronym LDRSHIP (Loyalty, Duty, Respect, Selfless Service, Honor, Integrity, and Personal Courage) is something I teach my students and use in the classroom every single day. My students understand how these things build good character, what the colors on the flag represent, why it is important to say the pledge, and why it is important to be thankful to the men and women who serve our country.

Service Learning is a huge part of my classroom. I believe that students learn more from doing and serving while connecting that to curriculum than they ever will just reading out of a textbook.

Veterans are very important to me. My students have knowledge that the freedoms they very much enjoy, including the education they receive,

S. FABIAN BUTALLA

are built on the blood, sweat, tears, and sacrifices of the men and women that are called to duty to protect the freedoms we have today.

I am proud of my military service. Although I didn't deploy, I still served my country. I still did things that helped my community and I was ready to go if called upon prior to meeting my husband and children.

***

It saddens me when I heard many of the stories of our women who have served but did not feel equal.

As a woman, while serving, I didn't feel "invisible" since our unit was like a family and the men around us were brothers and fathers, not superiors. We all pushed each other to do our best. But the day came when I signed the paperwork and turned in my things, and the feeling somewhat changed. There were some who understood my reasons for leaving and some that did not. I felt the stigma of one who was not fulfilling the duties I had sworn under oath to complete.

There have been many times that I entered a conversation when people have discovered that I am a veteran and they are surprised, often in disbelief. When they learn that I never deployed, their body language changes. Then I feel "invisible." There have been many veterans who have served during times of peace and never deployed, but they were ready to go when called. The stigma seems wrong.

The time I have felt the most "invisible" was this past Veterans' Day when I went to a popular restaurant with my grandfather to receive the free Veterans' Meal. It is an amazing event they sponsor and we saw veterans from all walks of life. When the bill came, they hadn't comped my meal. My grandfather made sure, in a stern voice, to explain that I was a veteran too. The server hadn't thought to ask. Many people do not view females as soldiers or veterans. We are child bearers and mothers. However, we can be both—and we are veterans as well.

My message to other American women is this: Do not let the fear of not being equal or good enough stop you from pursuing your dreams. If you pursue a dream and that dream changes

133

due to starting a family, do not feel guilty. If you have served, stand proud and own it. If something negative happened to you because you are a woman, speak out about it. Together we can change the world. Stand proud and tall. Know that you are not alone. And know that we are not invisible!

TWENTY-TWO

Mary Kay Olson

Flight Instructor Mary Kay Olson
US Navy, 1943-1945

*A*S IRISH IMMIGRANTS, my parents (from the Mooney and Rice families) sailed from Ireland and settled in Corning, Ohio. My life began in Corning on November 1, 1921. I came from a family of four brothers and two sisters.

Both of my grandfathers worked in the coal mines and my father became a mechanical engineer. He left the mines and started his own company called "Star Engineering" when we moved to New Lexington, Ohio in the 1930s.

I consider my upbringing as one that stressed responsibility, hard work, commitment, respect, and strong Irish values. Education was a door that opened and altered my life. I had to assert myself when asking my parents if I could go to college. My father was against any of his daughters attending college. He felt that college was for men and a woman's place was in the home, and my mother supported his position. I kept pushing my father to send me to college in Columbus. The argument I used was, Why could all of my brothers have the opportunity to go to college but not me and my sister?

I was relentless in my pleas and he finally conceded. In 1939 my parents allowed me to go to Columbus. After two years of secretarial courses, I planned to major in Literature and complete a four-year college degree at Ohio State University. However, on December 7, 1941, the Japanese attacked the US Naval base at Pearl Harbor, and one of my brothers joined the Army and another joined the Navy.

I continued my studies until July of 1943, when I too made the decision to enlist in the military. A friend from my hometown and I took a bus from New Lexington to Cleveland, where we both joined the Navy WAVES. I wanted to do something meaningful to contribute to the war effort and the WAVES seemed to be the best opportunity.

My mother was extremely upset and couldn't believe that I didn't ask for her approval. She found out in a local news article that I had enlisted. A few family members and friends were shocked. Only my sister Libby was excited for me and she also wanted to enlist in the WAVES. She asked our mother, who refused to allow her to do so.

I was twenty-two years old at the time of my induction into the WAVES. I was sent to WAVES boot camp at the USS *Hunter* (aka Hunter College Boot Camp in New York), located in the Bronx. It was here that we received basic instructions.

We also had to go through a battery of tests to determine our interests and qualifications. After testing I was asked if I would consider doing secretarial duties, and I said emphatically "NO! I want to do something in the area of aviation."

Based on my test score, I was one of two selected in our entire group to go to school in Atlanta, GA, where I was trained and became a Link Trainer Instructor.

In that position, I taught officers instrument flight training in the Navy's

Link flight simulators at Corpus Christi, TX. It was here that I found purpose. It was a very exciting time in my life, and yes, I taught men how to fly planes!

I received my Honorable Discharge in Corpus Christi, TX, on January 22, 1945, and I was married there to a Navy pilot, Glen. O. Olson. He was sent on active duty to the Pacific theater, stationed on Guam.

I moved to San Mateo, CA, awaiting my husband's return, while I was pregnant with twins that sadly died at birth. Adding insult to injury, only my husband's name along with our two daughters was on the gravestone. I had served our country, yet because I had been discharged, my name was left out. It added greatly to my grief, and it was the first time I ever felt "invisible."

***

I am proud and grateful to have served in the armed forces. It changed my life.

At the same time, it was the beginning of a new life with my husband and the family we created. I am now the proud mother of seven wonderful children, (five sons and two daughters)!

On November 1, 2018, I will have turned ninety-seven years old, and I am still thankful for the life I have lived over the decades.

Mary Kay Olson passed away on
April 12, 2019 at the age of 97.

TWENTY-THREE

Laura Rice

Petty Officer 3rd Class Laura Rice
US Navy, 1975-1981

I WAS A Baby Boomer, born in Minneapolis, MN, in 1955, and grew up in a family of eight kids. It was like living in a dorm room or boot camp. You had to forge a path for privacy to get what you wanted but still get along with the rest. I would sneak out in the morning before anyone else would wake up so I could have time to myself. My brothers, sisters, and I would run along the creek, hike up into the caves, make picnic lunches, go swimming, and explore. We had so much freedom, and we walked and biked everywhere. We had that false sense of freedom and did not feel the weight of a rule book upon us until I left home and my consequences of my action/reaction became my law.

My dad was in the Navy at the end of WWII, but never saw combat. We never really understood war until the '70s. The idea of being in the military was far away in my mind, and I was and still am so strongly against war.

Though I loved freedom, I sought out structure, which seems a strange bedfellow with my upbringing. I joined a group called the Minnesota Teen Corps when I was fifteen, and worked on building nature trails for physically and mentally-challenged residents of various state hospitals. We would camp out all summer with other teenagers, sing and dance with the State Hospital residents, and work hard. I decided to quit school in my 11th year of High School, and I lived on Teen Corps land, preparing for the hundreds of volunteers who would be coming for the summer to help build structures and places for the kids who were in the "system."

After that summer of working on the Cass Lake Indian Reservation in 1973 with Teen Corps, at seventeen I hitch-hiked to Boston to study natural food cooking with a Japanese family. I learned how to sew a kimono, cook great healthy food, and discovered a whole new way of looking at things through the view of another citizen of the world. I finished my GED and went through all of the "7th Inn Restaurant" phases of cooking, including: dishwasher, fry cook, short order, steam table/salad, baker, and chef. Two years later, I knew that I didn't want to be a cook. I also knew I didn't have enough money for college, and I didn't know enough about the world to feel comfortable. My co-worker at the restaurant where I trained was checking out the military service, so I did as well. I realized that this was what I should do and what I needed to fill in the blanks for my evolution and revolution of self to fix this world and make it a better place. I went to each of the forces and reviewed them, but in the end, I chose the branch my dad did. I loved water and anything to do with water. I thought it was the right fit for me.

So, in 1975 I joined the Navy. I think I shocked most everyone. I joined the military at a very unpopular time, from the ending of the Vietnam War, and most people just rolled their eyes in disbelief because what I believed in was not war, but Humanity, and that didn't seem to equate in most people's eyes then. My family never said much, except for my father, who was very surprised and proud. I went in the "Get in Quick Plan" and hoped to get to school later.

At that time, the military didn't know what to do with the many women enlisting. I was first sent to Basic Training on August 1, 1975 in Orlando, FL. I was one of sixty young women being taught all the tricks they used to change you from a civilian into a military individual. It was intense, funny, and interesting. I became the cadence caller when we marched, because we were always out of sync, so I just started singing, "Left, right, right your left. Look at us and what do you see? We're the best damn company." I got it from some movie.

I was sent from there to a WWII "Float 'n Dry" dock that was close to being haunted, in Little Creek, Virginia, where we got to hoist 100-pound bags of sand into the blaster, blast sand on the bottom of small ship vessels, then shovel all the used sand away. Lots of foul weather gear, shoveling, and climbing up and down many ladders. We once tipped a tugboat over inside the dry dock as we tried to bring it up on an especially stormy day and the ensign in charge nearly lost his position. It was the best place to learn about the real Navy, and I learned how to drive many different kinds of vehicles from a forklift to a tractor loading sand.

I also went to welding school before having the opportunity to choose another trade. I went from the east coast of Little Creek, VA, to San Diego, CA, for radioman training and learned how to type. From my cooking school to my military training, I had literally learned everything that was necessary to equip me to be competent and survive for a lifetime—and I was still only twenty-one!

I was able to request desired placement, and I put in for Kolsas, Norway; Brussels, Belgium; and Naples, Italy. The powers that be gave me Guam.

Though I cried when I found out after the training I was to be stationed in Guam, it became the greatest gift. I was assigned to a very remote section of the base with all men in a tiny space and afforded top security clearance for what we did— to this day I do not say. Some of the most important things that happen in one's life are not planned or sought after. This small but rich place rewarded me with scuba diving, hang-gliding, softball, karate, driving a motorcycle, Cessna training, and living with a Guamanian family on their "ranchero." And most incredibly, my son, Nolan, was born in Guam in 1978. I was always fortunate in finding great child care for Nolan on and off base while I was in the Navy. On Guam I found a wonderful Scottish woman who ran a day care while her husband worked with me at SPECOMMS. My four-year commitment was finished after Guam, but because of the baby, I thought about extending two more years and see what I could do. I put in for the same locations I had done before, and this time I was assigned to NATO duty in Kolsas, Norway.

I took my maternity leave and all my saved days, and traveled with my four-month-old son through Asia to Japan, Korea, Taiwan, Hong Kong, Thailand, Nepal, and India before stopping in Germany to visit my sister prior to arriving at my duty station in Norway. The most remarkable part of traveling with a baby is the universal language and care that is invoked. Being a mother with a baby opened up so many doors on that trip and so many cultural windows of kindness and sharing. Actually, it was a bit of the opposite welcoming I got when I arrived at the NATO base.

I was around a lot of "brass," and a single, breast-feeding parent was embarrassing to a few. It was a very difficult beginning, as I had to deal with another side of the military of which I had been unaware. When I first joined the service, I would even counsel others to apply themselves, like I did; go to college and take extra training, then you will always stay above water in the military's eyes. But then I learned what it is like to be on the other end. I discovered later that when they found out that I was a single parent, they had tried to change my orders, but I was already en route.

Norway was an amazing experience. I enjoyed working with the Brits and other countries NATO represented. I got to live on a Norwegian farm, and met so many wonderful friends that I have gone back often to visit them. When my two-years were finished, I was going to stay in the military, but I decided that six years was enough.

***

Since then, I have tried cooking again and being a "Big Sis" as well as a social worker. I went back to Europe with my son and traveled all over the continent, then to Ghana, Africa, doing "humanitarian" work and taking care of an orphanage as well as teaching kindergarten in the "bush" with a group called AMURTEL.

I returned to the States because I had three years to finish my teaching degree in Art before the GI Bill ended in 1989. That was also the year my adopted daughter, Ilithyia, was born and graced my life, and that of my then ten-year-old son, six months before I graduated.

I taught at many different schools, mostly alternative. I did the "Youth Build" project to reconstruct old houses with youth for low income families. I substitute taught a lot, which gave me more freedom to decline a teaching job if I had to stay home with the kids. I was a full-time teacher often enough and enjoyed teaching art, phys ed, cooking, and yoga, so I got to enjoy teaching all of my talents.

When my son went off to college, my daughter and I decided to go to Hawaii for two years. I taught ESL (English as a Second Language) there for the first year, then phys ed the second year, as well as substitute teaching and night art classes at my daughter's school.

After Hawaii, I renewed my Red Cross qualifications and became an instructor and disaster relief operator. I got many certifications along with being a teacher for the Professional Responder Emergency Road Vehicle (ERV) driver for disasters, and a Disaster Relief Supervisor.

Then my granddaughter was born, and I have been helping my daughter with her care and enjoying being a part of this wonderful new life unfolding. I have rented out my home to international students so I can be free to take care of my granddaughter while her mother works full-time.

I continue to do my artwork, write poetry, and a few years back, I finished writing and illustrating my children's book titled *A Star to the Stars*.

***

The Navy experience gave me the world view I so needed.

I know so many times that being in the military helped me to get the jobs I applied for. Getting thanks took many, many years later, and I never actually got honored until I was part of the Native American Dakota family, who accepted me, although I am white. I have had a long and strong desire for a deep connection with the Native American people, their culture, and beliefs. There were many times at ceremonies and pow wows that veterans were called to march first before "The People." They honored the military as the warrior, who puts one's self first to keep others from harm's way. It was an honor and a beautiful thing to have that recognition.

Yet, I believe it is myself that makes me feel "invisible" so many times. I just go the route without saying anything or talking about my service, because it is something I did, like the stories we all have. It was only until it was politically correct to thank veterans a few years back, that some of my friends and siblings said, "Thank you for your service."

It is why the "I Am Not Invisible" campaign was so wonderful. I truly enjoy sharing and talking with other veterans, both women and men. It is this comradery that is truly exceptional, and no matter how different your background, we are connected with our incredible common ground of service.

***

I would say this to all women: One of the greatest lessons I learned is that sometimes we need to get out of our own way and allow the best thing to happen, whatever comes our way, because it always does. Speak up, stand up, brave up to stand out. Recognize your worth and enjoy others, for they may be in your same shoes and in need of a helping hand of welcome. It is through this that I have found a way to get many of us "closet" military women out of the trenches and shedding the veil of "invisibility.

> *My message to other American women is this: The world is so full of amazing things on all sides and all views. Each of us has a story to tell. We all have something to learn from each other, and every one of us can heal and be healed as we pass this way—together. It is a great thing to have someone listen to us and share with others the "Wonderful Web We Weave as Women in this World."*

TWENTY-FOUR

Karen L. Shaw

SSGT Karen L. Shaw
US Marine Corps, 1982-1991

I WAS BORN in Wisconsin and raised in Apple Valley, MN. I was the youngest of three kids. My brother Curt and sister Sue always looked out for me. My dad worked as an engineer for the U.S. Bureau of Mines. He had served in the Air Force during the Korean Conflict, although he did not talk about his time in the service much. My mother was a stay-at-home mom. Supper was at 6:00 p.m. sharp every night. I assumed this was the life every kid had, but I remember someone making the comment, "You and your Beaver Cleaver family!" I took it as an insult back then, but I realize now just how lucky I was to have grown up in that kind of household.

I spent summers on my grandfather's cattle ranch in South Dakota, loving every minute of it—riding horses, swimming, and playing with my cousins. I was a quiet kid who enjoyed playing outside and being in nature.

My dad, Robert, was a kind, gentle man. He very seldom raised his voice and never inflicted physical punishment on us kids. When I misbehaved, he would just lower his voice and tell me how disappointed he was with me.

I believe I got a lot of my strength and independence from my mom, Shirley. She grew up as a farm girl and learned to be self-sufficient. What I thought was normal was anything but. My mom sewed all of my clothes as a kid, but didn't all moms? If something was broken, mom fixed it. She rewired the lamps and laid the carpet. But didn't all moms? What she didn't realize at the time, was that she was laying the groundwork for me to become a Marine. She taught me to be self-sufficient and take on challenges even if I was unsure of the outcome.

One of my most vivid memories as a child involves my sister, Sue. She was more than four years older than me and she liked to boss me around when our mom and dad were not there. One day, when I was seven or eight, I was sitting on the swing set right before a storm came. It was *extremely* windy out. I loved the wind blowing me higher and higher on the swing. Sue came outside and said it was too windy and I had to go in. I just kept going higher and higher on the swing. She kept saying that a storm was coming and I needed to get in the house. Of course, I refused. She then began screaming at me, saying she would tell if I didn't go inside with her. "*Fine!*" I yelled as I jumped off the swing and followed her. About ten seconds later, as I was walking up the hill into the house, an old oak tree, about seventy-five or eighty feet tall was blown over in the wind and smashed the swing set into what looked like a million pieces! It was crushed flat. Had Sue not been the bossy big sister, I would not be here today. We still joke about the "day she saved my life," but I have to admit it is true. I am still close to my sister. We have done many fun things together while growing up, like taking skydiving lessons together. Even to this day, we go to concerts and many other things together. I still look up to her as my hero.

I learned to be tough from my brother, Curt. Although he was eight years older than me, he let me play football, baseball, and games with all the neighbor kids. He always looked out for me and made sure I was safe. When he became commissioned with the United States Air Force, I was proud to give him his first salute!

I graduated from Apple Valley High School in 1980, and immediately after, I applied and was accepted to be an international exchange student. I spent that summer in a rural area of Kenya, Africa, living with a tribal family. I learned more about myself and life in general in those four months than I learned throughout the rest of my life.

After I returned home, I attended a local community college, and was studying to become a police officer. I then realized that I wasn't ready to do the "college thing." It was during this time that I became bored and began to explore my military options. I started researching the different branches of the service. I liked the idea that the Marine Corps was not only the smallest branch, but also the toughest. At that time in my life, I loved challenges, and I was ready for it. I knew right away that I wanted to be a Marine. My rationale for joining the Marines was "If I could do that, then I could probably do anything." I wanted to prove to myself that I was able to succeed in a predominately-male branch of the service and would be able to "keep up with the boys."

I was nineteen years old when I joined the Marine Corps. I was in for about ten years.

My mom and dad weren't real thrilled about it, and my father wanted me to explore other branches; however, I think he knew that once I had made up my mind to join the Marine Corps, nobody was going to change my mind.

I actually enjoyed Boot Camp in Parris Island, SC. This is the only place where women Marines attend Boot Camp, and it was gender-segregated. I was guaranteed at enlistment that I would be assigned as a Military Police Officer. The chaplain was male, but we never saw male recruits. Marine Corps Boot Camp is the only recruit training that is still segregated; however, some daytime training is conducted with male platoons. Yes, it was hard. Yes, I got yelled at (a lot). But I knew I was strong enough and tough enough to make it. I graduated "Molly Marine," which is an award given by your platoon mates as having the most *esprit de corps*. My platoon mates believed I set the example of having the most honor, courage, and commitment. Getting that award is a moment I will never forget.

After Boot Camp graduation, my Military Occupational Specialty (MOS) was Military Police (MP). At that time, MP school was in a transition from training at Fort McClellan, AL, to Lackland AFB, TX. As it happened, I fell in the summer of 1982 and did not have to attend formal training. Instead I received on-the-job training at Camp Le Jeune, NC, which is a beautiful base on the NC coast.

I loved it! I had a lot of responsibility and authority for a nineteen-year-old.

MP School was a joint-service school located at Lackland AFB, in San Antonio, TX. After attending numerous instructor courses, and being an instructor for a while, I reached Master Instructor status and was selected to be an instructor at MP school. Being a Marine on an Air Force Base was great! The majority of students were Air Force Security Police students. We usually had about ten Marines and there were usually about sixty to seventy Air Force students in the class. I enjoyed teaching immensely and was respected by both students and staff. I was successful as a teacher, and obtained the rating of Master Instructor. In the late 1980s, I was named Instructor of the Year, which was a great honor.

I spent my entire military career Stateside.

***

While in the Marine Corps, I got married and had my first child, Travis. I then realized that being a Marine and being a good mother was simply not going to work for me. I had orders to go to Japan. Even though I loved the Marine Corps and it had been good to me, I did not want to raise my son while traveling across the country. I decided it was time to get out and go back to Minnesota. I felt good about the time I spent in the Marine Corps. I enjoyed it very much and had many opportunities to travel and have fun. Had I been single, and not a mother, I truly believe I would have stayed in and made a career out of it.

After leaving the Marines, I moved back to Apple Valley, MN, and we bought a house just down the street from where I grew up. I finished college and used my Marine Corps training to become a police officer for the City of Apple Valley. While employed as a police officer, I was able to utilize my Marine Corps teaching experience. I spent nine years as a Drug Abuse Resistance Education (D.A.R.E) instructor. The rest of the time, I spent as a patrol officer, responding to calls from the public for service.

During this time, I had two more children. Kali was born in 1995. There had not been a pregnant officer in our department before me. I was worried since maternity job protection was not in place at that time. However, the city and the department were great and found many tasks I was capable of doing while I was pregnant.

My youngest daughter, Kelsey, was born in 1999. By then, many women had successfully worked for the police department while expecting a child. I am glad I was able to pave the way to make this happen.

After almost twenty-five years, an opening came up in our records division, and I decided to apply for the position and retire from active police duty. The Records Division was something I felt I could do well into my "golden years." I currently work in this position and I plan on staying there as long as possible. Even though I am no longer an officer, I still feel I am helping the public, as I have done all of my life. Behind my desk hangs my Marine Corps Boot Camp Graduation picture.

**

I am proud that I was in the Marine Corps. I attend local veterans activities whenever I can.

I recently attended the 100th Anniversary of Women Marines in Washington, D.C. It was great to meet women of all ages who have served our country. However, I still run into people who do not know that women can and do serve in the Marine Corps. I like to let people know I was a Marine, but sometimes they just don't believe it, and the feeling of "invisibility" enters.

One day, I was at a local Veterans Day celebration, and they were giving away small door prizes. My name was called, and I won a T-shirt. As I went forward to claim the prize, a woman came up to me and grabbed the T-shirt, yelling, "The prizes are for veterans only!" I was stunned. I then grabbed it back and politely informed her that I was a United States Marine! She turned away and stalked off.

Women have served in the military for over 100 years, yet many times, we are not given the respect and acknowledgment we deserve. I want people to realize that women in the military play an important role in the success of the mission. Women are now in most every occupational specialty and are succeeding at a high rate. We are not going away and will continue to increase in numbers.

My message to other American women is this: You can be whatever you want to be, and do whatever you want to do. Don't let anybody tell you anything different. We may have been ignored in the past, and made to feel "invisible," but not anymore. We are part of history, and we are not invisible!

TWENTY-FIVE

Elizabeth Skilbeck

Senior Airman Elizabeth Skilbeck
US Air Force, 2001-2005

$\mathcal{G}$ ROWING UP, I split my time between the suburbs of Minneapolis and small towns in Minnesota and Michigan. My parents got divorced when I was in second grade, and by fourth grade, I'd acquired four step siblings and a baby brother. It was a head-spinning amount of change in a short time, but I was fortunate to have other adults to rely on—aunts and uncles, and especially my mom's parents.

I was a good student and an athlete, but by no means a "goody-goody." Not that I was a bad kid, by any means—I just had a creative side. When a recruiter came to our high school, I raised my hand in the assembly and asked if we got to shave our heads. I thought it was a valid question! (I did, in fact, shave my head a few years later.)

From the first day of preschool most of my friends were boys. I had a couple close female friends, but played with boys at recess and was the only girl on my Little League team. I was active, athletic, and had a sense of humor that went over a lot better with boys. With my short hair and unique sense of style—Converse high tops with neon green laces in kindergarten—most adults assumed I was a boy.

Even into high school, after many tomboys turned girlier, I hung out with the guys and did "guy things." In rural Michigan where I attended senior high, "guy things" involved setting fires and blowing stuff up. Because we were out in the country, we advanced well beyond mailbox bombs and campfires. While there were never actually mailbox bombs, there were car fires, molotov cocktails, and experiments with black powder.

All of this was done on a very large piece of property owned by a friend, whose widowed mom was never home.

I thought about enlisting straight out of high school, but at the time, I was "in love" and wanted to see how that panned out. It didn't.

I spent a couple of years working at a print shop in the Minneapolis suburbs, wondering what I wanted to do next. My Papa— my mom's father— was my #1 cheerleader, even when the rest of my family lost patience with me. He'd tell me, "Women in your generation can do so much more than in the past, and with your brains you could do anything!" It took me a while, but finally I realized that what I wanted was to be more like him— the man I respected more than anyone. He'd served in the Navy in Korea, and remained in the Naval Reserve until retiring as a captain in 1985.

That's ultimately what led to my decision to join the military. My stepdad served in the Army, which he didn't think would suit me, and there was no doubt in my mind that I that I was *not* cut out to be a Marine. Although my grandfather and his father had been in the Navy, he didn't want his granddaughter in that branch, and I couldn't argue.

What ended up sealing the deal was when I went to the recruiter's office, the Air Force guy was wearing wide-wale cords and had his tongue pierced. This was a branch where I'd feel comfortable. I enlisted in April 2001 at age twenty-two. My parents cried, for different reasons. My mom and stepdad were thrilled; my dad and stepmom were less than.

I don't remember how my friends reacted, but they were probably pretty surprised, (if only because you can't smoke weed in the Air Force).

Like every other recruit, I took the ASVAB to determine what career tracks were open to me. All of them, it turned out. I decided I was going to be a crew chief on the heavy airplanes. Wherever my plane went, I would get to go. It would be my way of seeing the world.

That fell through when I got strep throat and didn't get to leave on my scheduled date. I could either wait several months until the next training class was available, or choose something else. I did something no one ever does, unless they're content to end up in Security Forces. I went to Basic Training without a designated career.

On the day that a few of us idiots without job guarantees went to fill out the paperwork to select a job, I said a little prayer. I asked what it was that I was supposed to do. Then I stepped out into the hallway and got my answer. On the wall near the drinking fountain, I saw pictures of robots, bombs, explosions, and all things that go boom. It was clear that Explosive Ordnance Disposal (EOD) was my answer. I selected the bomb squad. After all, I'd unknowingly been preparing for it all my life!

The following days were a blur of paperwork and security clearances. I told my family to expect to hear from the federal government about my background check.

When I told my mom what my job choice was, she said, "You get to blow shit up legally?"

I told her, "Yes! And they are going to pay me more to do it!"

My career training happened in two stages: the preliminary at Lackland, then the majority was at Eglin AFB in Florida.

This was a great spot to spend nine months of your life. Students from other branches and even other countries received their EOD training at Eglin. I met some interesting characters and enjoyed the nightlife, (a perk of already being in my twenties.) I also loved going to the Gulf of Mexico and watching stingrays ride the waves. I had no idea they liked to surf, or that they can jump!

I was in demolition training on 9/11. It was the most surreal day in my life. They called us all together, trainees and instructors, and told us about the events of that morning. We stood in a sea of camouflage in a parking lot, looking up at the Navy Commander on the flatbed of a truck, as he gave us all the details. I don't remember a thing he said. All I do remember was that he had a hula girl tattooed on his forearm. The idea of serving my country took on a new weight that day. Joining the service was no longer just a career path I'd chosen.

I was stationed at Hill Air Force Base in Utah. It is home to one of the largest test and training ranges in the country. It is a pretty great spot for an EOD tech to be. Pilots would run test missions, dropping inert munitions in the middle of the desert, then we would go out into the range and dispose of what they dropped. That was the busy work. The coolest part of our range mission was acting as glorified "garbage men."

We were also in charge of naval rocket motor disposal. We would place an explosive charge in the motor that needed to go away, detonate it, and end up with a gigantic hole.

These motors produced roughly a 200,000-pound detonation. You could see the sound wave coming before you could hear or feel it—and boy, did you feel it!

In the late spring of 2003, I was deployed to Saudi Arabia and the United Arab Emirates. In Saudi Arabia, I got to fly out to the middle of nowhere and disarm a warhead. While walking back to the helicopter, the Saudi Arabian pilot asked me if I could, "Leave base, for how you say, meals?" I couldn't. My team chief overheard the conversation. I never heard the end of it.

I got bitten by some bug in Saudi Arabia. I woke up with a bite on my shoulder and red lines webbing out from it, but no superpowers. I spent a few days on a serious antihistamine that knocked me on my ass. Doctors outlined the bite with a Sharpie and told me that if it traveled outside the line, I was going to get Medevac'd out. It didn't.

We were the cleanup crew when our tent city in Saudi Arabia closed down. Our job was to clean and ship all our equipment back to the States—without us. As the ranking Airman, I took another Airman, a Humvee, and a load of equipment to the Saudi fire station to hose down the Humvee and equipment as we didn't have the right tools in our tent.

When we got there, it was business as usual, for us and for them. When we drove up, there were about three men sitting out front. By the time I walked from the driver's seat, around the front to the tailgate, (with my 9mm on my hip) there were close to twenty men—all watching very carefully. It was an uncomfortable situation. We cleaned very quickly.

We were forward deployed to the United Arab Emirates. The UAE was pretty uneventful at that time. We were at an established base and spent most of our time sweeping vehicles and on "poolside duty." Can't really complain about that. Sitting poolside and playing cribbage. However, we weren't allowed to detonate anything. A previous EOD team had done a training shot during prayer time and forgot to alert the locals.

We did get to do a lot of fun things with our robot, testing its capabilities to the limit. For instance, we taught the base commander how to remotely pour a beer!

***

I was medically separated from the service in 2005. It was bittersweet. After shoulder surgery, I was no longer fit to do my job. They say you can't wear the bomb suit with a screw in your shoulder (even though bomb robots are full of screws.) There was no specific injury, no story of how I got hurt. My shoulder just wore out. I think it was due to repetitive use at range clearances, or maybe heavy lifting—nothing dramatic.

I was offered a desk job, but I said that wasn't what I signed up for. I felt "invisible"—like I got fired by my country!

I am proud of my service, even if most people assume that it was my husband who served. He did not. I was actually stationed with his sister. We blew up stuff together.

She introduced us and told me, "This is my brother. You're going to marry him." And I did! We are now thirteen years and two kids into it. I wouldn't change a thing.

Today, I wear many hats. I am the stay-at-home mother of two, a private tutor, and a professional volunteer.

I try to stay active and highly engaged with the veteran community. I was awarded the first Fellowship from The Mission Continues for any veteran in Minnesota in 2012. During my six-month Fellowship, I worked with the Habitat for Humanity ReStore. When The Mission Continues, TMC, launched their service platoon program in 2014-15, I was able to fill a leadership role as squad leader in various positions to include the platoon's communication, outreach, and support event planning roles.

The service platoon was doing so well that they decided to launch a second platoon in the Twin Cities, and I was handpicked to be the platoon leader! I was able to partner with the St. Paul City School and tackle projects to help fill the needs of a school in the St. Paul Promise neighborhood. It was a very meaningful two years that I will never forget. My kids would get mad if they thought I was off to a service project without them. Proud Mom moment there.

That is my new mission— to make sure I am raising good people.

***

I am being reminded, not so subtly, that my presence in the veteran community has been recognized in several ways. I was nominated and recognized by The Mission Continues and NBC as part of a campaign honoring women warriors for the premiere of the short-lived show *American Odyssey.*

I was one of seven veterans selected to be interviewed and filmed by Minnesota Twin Cities Public Television to tell my story of service for Public Service Announcements that were broadcast on Public Television. I have to admit, that one was kind of fun. My kids sure liked having the camera crew with us at the park.

I was also a recipient of a Veterans' Voices "On the Rise" award in 2015.

Service has always been a part of who I am. I try to keep it a part of my daily life. The way I serve may be different, but why I serve will always be the same. Family. It started because of my Papa. It continues because of my kids. I want to set the example for them that he set for me.

***

I was super excited when Minnesota released the Women Veteran license plate. It has reduced the number of times I have felt "invisible" after being told to thank my husband for his service. It is easy to feel overlooked as a woman veteran. The assumption is always that veterans are men.

I would serve again, but I really don't want my kids to do it.

My message to other American women is this: Live your dream. You can be tough, but whatever you do, don't lose your sense of humor! I got paid to ride on a four-wheeler with C-4 in my backpack!

Special thanks to my sister Jannette Peterson for her assistance.

WE ARE NOT INVISIBLE

TWENTY-SIX

Julie A. Williams

GYSGT Julie A. Williams
US Marine Corps, 1978-1999

W HEN I WAS in the fifth grade, I was adopted. With the exception of going for ice cream with the social worker, I don't remember it being such a big deal. My birth family knew my adopted family. We had been neighbors actually. This was the late '60s and families were changing. The four of us kids were moved and passed around a bit before my younger sister and I were quite literally dropped off at the neighbors' house.

Fortunately, they knew us and loved our family in spite of the troubles, and they later adopted us. I then became the fifth child out of seven; just an average middle child trying to get along. I don't recall being particularly outgoing; maybe even more of a follower than anything else—with a little bit of a planner tucked deep inside. One time I planned a neighborhood kids Halloween party (just because I thought it would be fun) and never mentioned it to my parents ahead of time!

Life was typically suburban: father worked and mother stayed home; school was important and good grades were expected; neighborhoods were safe and kids were constantly out playing together. It was Midwestern American living.

I began making my own friends when I started high school (other than those in the neighborhood). I liked school but got only average grades. I don't remember it being difficult, but it was mostly just my *laissez faire* attitude at that time. I tried a couple of athletic activities but found out I wasn't very good at them. I did, however, participate in some support/cheer clubs.

I pretty much bought into what was expected for my life—do what you're told and stay out of trouble. I thought I was doing okay. But as graduation got closer, I wondered what I was going to do with the rest of my life. A few of my friends had plans for college, and I even took the entrance exams, but really didn't know what I wanted out of life. Other than delivering newspapers, I still never even had a real job. I also knew my family couldn't afford to pay for college.

My three older brothers had all enlisted in the military, but I thought—ugh!—not for me. Reality hit when lack of funds with no concrete plan left me with few options. So I took a job in a local plastics factory working on the assembly line, third shift, and borrowing rides from anyone who would take me there.

I finally decided that I needed something more. I didn't know what it was or even how to get there, but I knew I had to go. To my surprise, the Marine recruiter was willing to pick me up and talk about options. My mother had told my brother's recruiter that I was the one he really should be pursuing. "Ha, I thought, never in a million years!" The following month, I was standing on the yellow footprints!

My father had been a Marine during WWII and Korea, but there wasn't much talk about it. I don't think I chose the Marine Corps over any other branch for any reason than the Marine recruiter had been the latest one to visit our house.

My brother who was still in the Marines was excited that I was joining the Corps. The others were in the Army and Navy, so they just wished me well. My parents were happy for me. I still have the good luck note and gift my youngest brother left on the table for me the morning I left. (Four years later, he too joined the Marines.) I had signed the papers with my recruiter in February of 1978, and was eighteen and a half when I was ordered to report in March for Boot Camp in Parris Island, SC.

The night before reporting for Boot Camp, I had celebrated St. Patty's Day with my older sister and an aunt (yup, using a fake ID), and other than showing up with green painted fingernails, I don't remember too much of the plane ride to Parris Island, SC. Once there, the geography was so different from Minnesota in March. There was lots of talk and laughing on the bus until someone mentioned swamps and alligators. Reality was starting to set in.

Parris Island was nothing like one might imagine from its name. I know I wasn't physically prepared for Boot Camp, and probably not mentally either. I was now living, eating, running—everything with forty-eight other women on a very strict schedule, and for what? This was a place where all kinds of classes and training were thrown at us and at times I wondered for what purpose. We were issued uniforms and they were worn as an outward sign of how we would lose who we were individually. We were becoming Marines who would act and react in very structured and expected ways.

Remember, this was the late '70s and the Cold War was in play. We were part of a military institution that had traditions and standards and needed to be ready if the call ever came in.

We were still women and because of that, our training differed from that of the men. We were issued different types of utility uniforms (no boots); we did not qualify with weapons, and we didn't even participate in obstacle training activities. Instead, we were given lessons in make-up, hosted a tea for some of the officers and their wives, and even had a field trip to a historical town which we toured and then stayed for dinner. Did I mention sand fleas?!

I had enlisted under Open Contract, meaning the Marine Corps would assign me where needed. At the time, very few areas were available to women regardless of your ASVAB test scores. So after Boot Camp, I was assigned to Basic Administrative School and did well enough to be promoted after graduation.

Three years later I went on to an advanced administrative class, a school normally attended by those on second or subsequent enlistments. Academically I did well and received a Proficiency grade of 5.0 (the highest score.) My Conduct grade, however, was only 4.6. Perhaps I had a bit of an attitude.

I was also able to attend a senior Leadership Academy at my fifteen-year mark. This was a great opportunity to work more closely with my peers to develop more personally.

For most of my career (1978-1999), I was assigned to non FMF (non-deploying) units and for this reason primarily, I never deployed. I did spend one year unaccompanied (without family) on Okinawa, Japan, but of course, this was not during war time. I knew that my "number" would eventually come up for these kinds of orders, and it was somewhat stressful. When I was thirty-two, I had a twelve-year-old daughter. I faced the question: "What kind of woman would leave her family behind?"

Why is it so horrible for a woman to transfer when duty calls, yet for most men it is considered normal and his family supports his decision for keeping his career on track?

I was initially assigned to one of the permanently-based support squadrons, but within a couple of months was reassigned to the Group headquarters. This was based on my job skills, but I'm sure my gender had something to do with it too. I was the Administrative Chief in the Adjutant's office (who was only a 2nd lieutenant) and we also had two clerks. We handled all the paperwork for the Group Commander, who was a colonel.

As a staff NCO, I was housed in a barracks with even fewer women, so making friends was not always easy. It was not uncommon for gossip to be started when people had the most innocent relationships. I was able to get a driver's license and a car, so I became more mobile, got more friends, and enjoyed more of the island.

Yes, at times there was and is some feeling of "invisibility." The military, and especially the Marine Corps, has far more men than women serving or have served. Yes, I was a Marine, but I am still a woman—a capable woman who applied what I was taught and was able to "hold my own." I continued to work at excelling in some areas that I was already good at, and of course did what needed to be done to improve in others that didn't come naturally for me (i.e. physical training).

I knew that just based on my gender, I was different, but by being myself and the best Marine I could be, I was going to keep in step and be just as valuable as the rest of my peers. Were there times when I wasn't the first one selected for something? Probably.

But there were other times when I was able to lead in my own style and handle situations as I thought best. For example, there was an incident on Okinawa where a young, troubled Marine was struggling with his gender identification and had to be placed in the base hospital on suicide watch. I'm not sure where the line was for me between mother and leader while I was involved with this, and I'm not sure that it really mattered. It's all part of who I am. I learned to be strong and value who I am - and to use my gifts accordingly.

As I was approaching my twenty-year mark, my daughter was a junior in high school. I couldn't make her switch schools one last time, so I opted to stay and request permission to retire the following year. My daughter graduated in May of 1999, and in July, after twenty-one years of service, at the age of forty, I retired from the Marine Corps. Some might say it was a formidable accomplishment; for me it all just went by so quick. I have so many great memories—the people, the places, just so much. I rarely, if ever, think about those who were unkind or tried to hold me back. I was lucky to be able to serve and will remain grateful for the opportunity.

As I drove away, headed for home, Quantico, VA, was in my rearview mirror and I was ready to move on—or so I thought.

Of course, I had attended my requisite retirement classes before I left and believed I was capable or experienced enough and maybe even young enough to start another career. But shortly after unpacking and rearranging things, I found myself just sitting on the couch—yes, literally sitting on the couch. "Now what?" was my daily thought. I had just left being a part of something that was so much bigger than myself; something where my name wasn't really that important. It was my uniform. It was who I was and what I did for twenty-one years, and all of a sudden I wasn't wearing that uniform any more. Now what?

I had to realize that it was up to me to find my new place. I joined a women veterans' organization, found part-time work, and went back to my hobbies. I had to find me—just without a uniform.

***

Even though I did not serve during a time of war or engage the enemy in combat, I believe my service still had honor. I believe that my service gave respect to those who paved the way which allowed me to enlist and my service proved that the value of women in the military is still warranted.

I had signed up for something constructive in my life, and I ended up staying for twenty-one years. I wanted to find something more for myself. And that I did. In addition to a few good men, I also met a few very good women, many with whom I am still in contact. There is a deep sense of camaraderie in military service, an incredible bond that is almost impossible to explain.

Despite the many shapes and sizes that we come in, what we know on the inside, our common knowledge of where we have been will forever keep us connected. I was part of something great, and I earned my eagle, globe, and anchor. I know that "Once a Marine, always a Marine." I am truly grateful that I was able to serve.

***

No one who has or is serving in our country's Armed Forces should ever have to feel "invisible." When most people discover that I did serve, and if they offer a "Thank you for your service," my most frequent reply is, "It was my pleasure." I have now been retired for almost as long as I served and still find it amazing that people are surprised that I am a veteran. Perhaps I don't fit the image— but there shouldn't be one! The contributions of women veterans are as varied as the women who have served, and I'm proud to be included with all of them.

I just hope there is appreciation for *all* of those who served, regardless of who, when, or where—an appreciation and an understanding of the military service and sacrifices that are made when anyone commits to the service of his or her country.

My message for other American women is this: Take a chance. Life is full of choices and distractions but we can only find out what's really out there for us when we take a chance. I'm not the same person I was in 1999 when I retired, and definitely not that young girl at eighteen who left for military recruit training. But I am happy with my life.

Yes, I've taken chances. No, I am not invisible!

INVISIBLE SOLDIER
Sarge Lintecum © 1995

You can tell her by the twinkle in her eye,
at parades when the flag marches by.
She served our country and she served it very well.
Some have even served a tour or two in Hell.

She suffered hardship and never ceased to care.
It gave us strength just to know that she was there.
She was a leader, you could tell by the rank she wore,
But she became the invisible soldier after the war.

She can march, she can fly, and she can sail.
She proved that bravery isn't exclusive of the male.
She did every job she was asked and more,
But she became the invisible soldier after the war.

Now it is finally time to right a wrong.
Honor our sister soldier; hear her song.
It's very clear that she's a patriot to the core.
Don't let her be the invisible soldier anymore.

This poem is cast in bronze and stands beside the Arizona Women Veterans' Memorial at the Arizona National Memorial Cemetery in Phoenix, Arizona. Sarge Lintecum unveiled it on Memorial Day in 1996 at the Memorial Day Veterans' Ceremonies.

Glossary of
Military Acronyms Used

APFT	Army Physical Fitness Test
AMEDD	Army Medical Department
AWOL	Absent Without Leave
AIT	Advanced Individual Training
ASVAB	Armed Forces Vocational Aptitude Battery Test
ALO	Air Force Liaison Office
AFB	Air Force Base
BOLC	Basic Officer Leader Course
BCT	Basic Combat Training
BLT	Battalion Landing Team
CAB	Combat Aviation Brigade
CO	Commanding Officer
CQ	Charge of Quarters duty
C2	Plastic explosive
CID	Criminal Investigation Division
DFAC	Dining Facilities (chow hall)
DERO	Date Eligible for Return from Overseas
EOD	Explosive Ordnance (bomb) Disposal
ESL	English as a Second Language
ERV	Emergency Road Vehicle
FMF	Non-deploying units
FOB	Forward Operating Base
GRE	Graduate Record Exam
INF	Infantry Division
IRR	Inactive Ready Reserve
KP	Kitchen Patrol
LDAC	Leadership Development and Assessment Course
MAC flight	Discount airfare for veterans

MOS	Military Occupational Specialty (job training)
MST	Military Sexual Trauma
MWR	Morale, Welfare, and Recreation
MEB	Medical Evaluation Board
MEPS	Military Entrance Processing Station (all branches)
MEU	Marine Expeditionary Unit
MRE	Meal Ready to Eat
MSG	Marine Security Guard
NBC	Nuclear, Biological, Chemical warfare
NCO & NCOIC	Non-Commissioned Officer in Charge
NSTP	Nurse Summer Training
NVGs	Night Vision Goggles
OIF	Operation Iraqi Freedom
PT	Physical Training (exercises)
PSYOPS	Psychological Operations
PEB	Physical Evaluation Board
PTSD	Post-Traumatic Stress Disorder
ROTC	Reserve Officer Training Corps
RN	Registered Nurse
TCT	Tactical Team

A Note from Photographer Dallas Smith

*I*N THE SPRING of 2017, my good friend, the late Bridget Cronin, talked with me about her desire of starting an I Am Not Invisible project here in MN and asked if I would consider being involved. She asked if I would be willing to put time into talking with the women and trying to capture their individual personalities in portraits. I loved the idea and was excited at having the opportunity to use my skills to give back to others while support and bringing awareness to the vast contributions of female veterans. While I have not been in the military, I was raised to understand and respect the sacrifices the our veterans and their families make in order to keep us all safe. My grandfathers both served during World War II, one in the Marines and the other in the Air Force. Through being involved in this project, I have also been blessed with developing very dear friendships with a few of the women in this book. And all of the female veterans in this book have been beyond gracious, welcoming, genuine, and truly inspirational to me.

I hope that reading their stories will also be just as inspirational to you. It is truly an honor to be a part of this project.

—Dallas Smith

About the Author

S ANDRA FABIAN BUTALLA was born and raised in Toledo, Ohio; graduated from Bowling Green State University; taught junior high school English in Oregon, Ohio, and Los Angeles, California; and taught senior high school English and College Writing at schools in northern Minnesota. She then served as K-12 Media Director for five schools within the St. Louis County Schools District of northern Minnesota, to-taling more than thirty-two years of service in the field of education.

She is the author of *The Man Who Fell to Earth*—the amazing true story of World War II flyboy Robert Givens and his harrowing fall from a B-17 at 20,000 feet over the North Sea.

Her second book is *Warbirds in the Cloak of Darkness*, which tells the incredible true story of American Airman Robert Holmstrom and the highly-dangerous top-secret missions he flew for the OSS during World War II. Ms. Butalla currently lives in northern Minnesota with her family.

To my 26 "Soldier Sisters," and to all of our women veterans, I wish to say: May you never feel "invisible" again. Thank you for your service!

Also by the Author

THE MAN WHO FELL TO EARTH

*The Incredible True Story of
WWII Flyboy Robert Givens*

The compelling true life story of a World War II airman, his harrowing fall from a B-17 as it broke apart over the North Sea, and the life he lived in the years that followed.

*ISBN: 978-1-55571-844-2 (Paperback)
174 pages • $14.95*

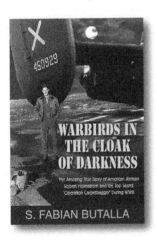

WARBIRDS IN THE CLOAK OF DARKNESS

The Amazing True Story of American Airman Robert Holmstrom and the Top Secret 'Operation Carpetbagger' During WWII

Follows the dangerous, highly secret "Carpetbagger" missions, whose participants were sworn to secrecy for forty years after WWII.

*ISBN: 978-1-55571-921-0 (Paperback)
230 pages • $14.95*

*Available on Amazon.com and other online booksellers,
through Barnes & Noble and your favorite bookstore,
or direct from Hellgate Press at www.hellgatepress.com*

Help is Out There

*I*F YOU ARE a woman veteran, or if you know someone who is, the U.S. Department of Veterans Affairs is there to help.

Within the VA is a designated department which is dedicated to meeting the needs of women veterans at all stations of their military service.

Some of the numerous ways they are prepared to offer services include: transition assistance and community integration, benefits and resources available, social and emotional health resources, home loans, and education benefits.

For information on the services and assistance available to women veterans, visit the following website:

https://www.womenshealth.va.gov/WOMENSHEALTH/
programoverview.about.asp

In addition, there is the "Women Veterans Call Center," where a woman veteran's issues will be addressed by a team of people who are anxious and able to help. Call or text the following number: 1-855-829-6636.

Another fast and easy way to make contact with the many people and organizations that can provide assistance in several ways is to visit the following Veterans Resources website:

https://www.womenveteransinitiative.com

You Are Not Alone!